MW01267840

TORN BETWEEN TWO LOVERS

TWANA JOYNER-NUNISS

God's Way Publishing

Unless otherwise stated, my scriptural quotations in this volume
are from the King James Version of the Bible.

For further information contact:
God's Way Publishing
twananuniss@gmail.com

Cover Design by Fredrick Buffington and The Buffington Effect
Marketing Solutions
Interior design by Borel Graphics
Edited by Twana Nuniss and Andrea Robinson

Printed in the United States of America
ISBN 13: 978-1-5448-3316-3
22 21 20 19 18 17   6 5 4 3 2 1

Thank You's

First of all, thank you Father God for the awesome opportunity and gift that you have given me to write and publish books! I am both thankful and humbled. I would also like to thank all the of the wonderful people that purchased my first book, *"Looking for Love in all the Wrong Places"* and those who came out to witness the book come to life in the form of "Looking for Love-The Play". Thanks to all the gracious churches that allowed me to hold book signings and to share with their congregations such as Longley Baptist Church, Grace Temple, St Mark, Abundant Life and so many others. Although the book took longer than it should have to get here in my eyes, I still believe that it is right on schedule according to God's plan.

Thank you Candy Taylor for being my friend, my sister-cousin, my ride or die chick and everything else that I have needed you to be. You stuck with me the entire time we were traveling with the play, assisted me with book signings and helped me set up for events. You keep me motivated and can always make me laugh. I just want you to know that I appreciate everything that you have done.

Thanks to my co-editor, Andrea Robinson (grandma in the play) for stepping in and helping me with the editing. God knew what He was doing when He chose you.

Thanks to Denise Billups of Borel Graphics in Chicago, Illinois for the design and layout, Fredrick Buffington of the Buffington Effect Marketing Solutions in Little Rock, Arkansas for the cover design and Andrea Robinson for co-editing. I appreciate all of your hard work.

Readers, please note that just as before, many of the names have been changed to protect the innocent and not so innocent; God knows the difference.

denotes a fictitious name

*D*edications

I would like to dedicate this book to my children, Corey, Tashona, Katecia and Jeremiah and the newest additions to our family, my grandchildren, Keortnay (Jeremiah), Khloe (Corey) and Jonah (Tashona).

I also dedicate this book to my mother Ora London and my grandmother, Cora Joyner. God knew what it would take for a child like me so he gave me an awesome balance of mothering between the two of you. Love you much!

Last but not least, I would like to dedicate this book to my guardian angels, my father, Edward L. London Sr., who went to be with the Lord in 2013 and my baby brother, Courtney W. London, who went to be with the Lord in 2014. It's still hard to believe that the two of you are gone. I thank God for being able to find peace in knowing that to be absent from the body is to be present with the Lord. The selfish part of me wishes you were still here, but in my heart I know that you could not be in a better place. Until we meet again—rest in love.

Preface
TORN BETWEEN TWO LOVERS

Torn between Two Lovers is the continuation of my personal story and just as before, I keep it 100! I share the good, the bad and the ugly; the call on my life does not give me any other options. My belief in what God ordained me to do compelled me to write and my convictions would not allow me to compromise. My prayer is that someone will gain insight from my struggles and successes and be encouraged to stay in the race.

During the writing of this book it became even more evident to me that many of the things that I desired for my life were not in the cards. Although I was saved and filled with the Holy Spirit, I struggled and continue to struggle with certain issues during certain seasons in my life. During some of my hardest times, God told me just as He told Paul, "My grace is sufficient." Although I will never be okay with my shortcomings, I have become okay with my process.

Torn between Two Lovers confirms what sinners already believe about saints. We really don't have it as together as we appear to and fall short in our walk with God more often than we care to admit. There were times I almost lost my mind, literally, yet God steadied me and did not allow the enemy to take it. I found myself torn between my love for God and the things that my flesh still had a liking for. "But God !"

The great Donnie McClurkin has a song and one line of the lyrics say "a saint is just a sinner who fell down, and got up". I think that's an awesome analogy of who a Christian really is.

I thank God for exchanging His beauty for my ashes, for

hearing my cry in my darkest hours and for lifting up my head when I felt down trodden. I thank Him for being with me in my loneliest times, for guiding me when I did not have direction and for providing for my every need.

The bible says that God reigns on the just as well as the unjust, therefore we should not be envious of the sinner that is forgiven and blessed by God. Truth be told, sinner or saint, we are all struggling with something and if God don't fix it, it won't get fixed.

I pray that something in my story will cause you to realize that God loves you more than you could ever imagine, He desires for you to be free in all aspects of your life and He is truly a just, loving and forgiving God. Be Blessed!

Foreword

BY ORA D. LONDON

As a young girl I was gifted on February 18, 1964 with a bundle of joy. She was my joy then and is my joy now. Though the road was not always easy for me or her , we both have moved forward, got things right that tried to drive us apart and allowed God to bond us together greater than ever before.

There were times that I saw Twana going through some things that others could not have made it through and keep their sanity, but God graced her and she continued to bring glory to His name by standing in faith. I could not be prouder.

One thing that I know for sure is that Twana loves her family and seeing them happy. Her hot off the press prayers pierces the heart and calms the soul of those that hear them.

Just like you, I am looking forward to reading "Torn between Two Lovers". I can only imagine what it took to put all of her business out there again for all to read, but God has never led her wrong.

Twana, through the good times and the bad times, I will continue to stand by your side. The joy that you have, the world did not give it to you and the world cannot take it away.

With love, your mom

Prayer of Salvation

*F*ather God, in the name of Jesus, I acknowledge that I am a sinner. I ask that you forgive me of my sins and cleanse me from all unrighteousness. You said in Your Word that whosoever shall call upon the name of the Lord, shall be saved. I believe that you died for my sins and after 3 days you rose with all power in your hands and now sit at the right hand of the Father. I further believe that salvation is a gift and that there is nothing that I can do to earn it, but that it is given freely by You. I accept this gift and surrender myself to You as Lord of my Life. Help me to serve you in Spirit and in truth. In Jesus name I pray. Amen!

My Prayer for You

$\mathcal{L}$ord I thank you for those that have sown into my ministry by purchasing this book. I pray that you return their seed to them 100 fold. I pray for their families and that all of their needs will be met. Lord I pray for deliverance for those that need deliverance and peace to those who seek peace. I pray that my testimony will cause unbelievers to believe and believers to rejoice in knowing that you are a forgiving and loving God. Lord please continue to lead us in the paths of righteousness for Your name sake and keep your angels encamped around us and our families. I claim it to be so in Jesus name, Amen.

Table of Contents

denotes a fictitious name in order to protect identity

Torn Between Two Lovers

Chapter I

ℋeaded Back South
(Excerpt from final chapter of
Looking for Love in all the Wrong Places)

𝒫rior to going into the hospital I had come to realize that things between Solathian and I were not working out but I refused to believe it, mainly because of the new prophecy I had received. While pregnant, I had visited a church with Karan and some other ladies when a lady came to me and began to prophesy. She said "you and your husband are going to get back together and it is going to better than it ever was before". The last prophecy that I had received had been so accurate that I wanted this one to also be true. As everything seemed to be going contrary to the prophecy, I began to reflect on how Solathian and I initially got together. I had been married and cheated on my first husband and now all of the things I done to him were being done to me. Payday had finally come and it took me a while to realize that the seeds I had sown had once again sprung up. I knew that the only way the two of us would be together was if God did it so I decided to leave Germany and return to the states in order to be able to clear my head and to see if our relationship was really meant to be.

I prayed about it constantly and when I finally felt peace about it, I began preparing for the move. I called base housing and set an appointment for housing to pick up the furniture. I also called transportation to schedule the car being shipped and last but not least, I got assistance form Solathian's commander in getting orders for tickets to fly home to Arkansas. I don't know why Solathian would not help me get what I needed to go home but when I told him I was leaving, he let me know that he was not going to help me leave. I don't know if he was just being mean or if he just liked the idea of having his cake and eating it too. I was able to use some of my connections to get what I needed. I had to wait until Jeremiah turned one month old before they would let us fly. It would be a long 14-16 hour flight with four children aged 13,11,5 and 1 month. I wasn't looking forward to it but I knew I had to do it. I had good children so I did not forsee any problems. Prior to me leaving I went to Pastor Fitzgerald's church. Pastor Fitzgerald was once a member of Patton Christian fellowship and was also a dentist in the Army. He started a bible study that eventually led him to starting a church. We called it the "upper room" and Karan, her husband Will and some more of us had all ended up joining. It was much smaller than Patton but Pastor Fitzgerald was an awesome teacher and Pastor.

The Sunday before we were to leave, Jeremiah got christened and the church had also collected a love offering for me and the children. As I said, it was a very small congregation but that day, Pastor Fitzgerald gave me a plaque for working with the youth ministry and an envelope that had $1,000.00 cash in it. I will never forget the way they blessed me and my children and I know that God blessed them for that. Transportation came and got the last of our things on Monday, Solathian stopped by briefly a few days and was surprised to see that the house was empty except for the furniture that belonged to housing. It was an awkward moment as he kissed Katecia and Jeremiah and gave Corey and

Shona hugs. I held back the tears and he quickly left after he and I shared a slight embrace. That night was the last night that we would spend in Heidleberg Germany. So much had happened in such a short time it seemed.

The next day the children and I got in the car with Karan and Will and headed to the airport in Frankfurt Germany on our way back south. I did not see Solathian that day; I figured it was probably best. But as we headed toward that airport and I looked at my children, a sense of peace came over me and I knew that we would be okay. God had brought us too far and had showed us so much love through so many people. After a teary good bye we boarded the plane. I would miss Karan and my spiritual family in Germany but I remembered what Karan had told me. She said "God has grown you up fast in him and you are going to be fine as long as you continue to pray. Everything you need is already inside of you."

As I lay my head back on the headrest and prepared for the long flight, I tried to see my friends Karan and Will leaving the airport parking lot but I couldn't. I almost felt like grabbing the children and running off the plane because for a brief moment I felt totally lost. I was about to start my life all over again with 4 children, no job or place to stay that I could call my own. Before the thoughts could overtake me, I began to think of how God had shown his love toward me. God had used Pastor Fitzgerald and my church family to show me and my family love by blessing us monetarily. I also thought of "the bishop" and Pastor Boswell who had not only shown my family love, but had also played a major role in teaching us the Word of God. But what I thought of most of all was how all those years I had been looking for love in all the wrong places. I looked for it in people, in things, in alcohol and in drugs. I did not realize that in order to truly experience true love I had to first find it inside of myself. When I began to love my "temple" that is when my life began to change. Were things perfect? No. Were things hard at times? Yes. Did I want to give up, almost give up or gave up if only for a moment? Yes.

But the one thing I did not do is stop believing in the power of God. I know now that when there is a man in my life, God loves me, when there is no man in my life, God loves me, when I have money, God loves me, when I don't, God still loves me. I know God will never cheat or leave me and I know I can call him day or night and he will be there. I don't have to smoke weed to experience him and I don't have to drink to keep him. I know now that all the love I could ever need or want is in GOD. There is nothing that I can do to earn it because He gives his love freely; with no strings attached.

I wish that I could say that when I arrived down South that everything was perfect and I never made another mistake and that I was so saved and Holy Ghost filled and had it all together. NOT. What I did have however, was power. When I got saved God gave me the power through prayer to fight the enemy. Trust me when I say, everything God placed inside of me, was soon put to the test...

Psalm 28:7

"The Lord is my strength and my shield; my heart trusted in him, and I am helped: therefore my heart greatly rejoiceth: and with my song will I praise Him."

Square Numero Uno

When we landed in Little Rock my brother Keith picked us up from the airport. It was so great seeing him again. Before I left for the military we would hang out together in Stuttgart since we both had acquaintances there. Though we got along fine for the most part throughout our childhood, at that time he became my confidante and road dog.

I initially left Arkansas in 1982 thinking I would make Louisville my home but that didn't work out. Then I thought I would make the military a career so I enlisted in 1986 but that didn't work out the way I thought either. Although going back home was not an easy thing to do, I knew that God had led me back there–my plans and His plans were not the same plans. Looking back caused me to realize how time had flown by. So many things in our lives had changed. He was living in Little Rock and quickly moving up the ranks in management for a food chain. He was married and had one son, Tyler. I, on the other hand, had been out of the military for 4 years and was unemployed, recently separated from my husband and had 4 children. I remember thinking back to when I first left Arkansas. I thought that I had it all figured out. Admittedly, on the ride down home I realized that just like back then, I still had not figured out what "it" was. There were only a few things that I knew for certain in that moment and that was, I needed to find a job and I needed to find a place to stay and I needed to do them both expeditiously.

As Keith drove we shared fond memories of our childhood growing up in the country. Neither of us knew back then that the upbringing we had would not only prepare us for our stints in the military, but for life. We came from a community where everyone knew everyone and was related to mostly everyone. I can't speak for him, but as for me, meeting, trusting and adapting to other people's beliefs and lifestyle choices proved to be a bit hard for me to adapt to in the beginning. Eventually, I began to let my guard down and began to simply accept people for who they were. Because of that, I was able to establish some friendships that still exist to this day. You never know who or what God is using to help prepare you for life. Your experiences and encounters with certain people will undoubtedly be used as vehicles to catapult you into your destiny.

The hour and a half ride from Little Rock to Dewitt seemed extra-long due to my jetlag. The children slept as we rode and all I could think about was lying prostrate on somebody's bed. As I stared out the window looking at crop field after crop field, I could not believe that I was back where I started. I must admit, I felt like I did when I returned home from Louisville—defeated.

As the ride continued, I began to think about Solathian. I wondered what he was doing and who he was doing it with. I concluded that he was probably doing what he always did and was with whomever he wanted to be with—he had it like that. Although I did not have any control over what he was doing, I knew for certain that he would not be able to "do it" in the military quarters that our family once called home. I'd made it my business to completely clear all of the furniture out before I left.

It wasn't long before we were on Cedar Circle and I was looking my grandmother and grandfather in the face. It had been almost 3 years since I last saw them and my Aunt Bertha. It was so great seeing how God had kept them in such good health over the years. After loving on them for a while and catching up, Keith, myself and my crew headed over to my mom's apartment where she was busy tending to my baby sister's hair.

Unfortunately, my mom (Ora) and stepfather (Lewis) had divorced while I was away. It was hard to imagine them apart after so many years of marriage but they were living separate lives and were in relationships with other people. My sister was now a full grown woman and was expecting her first child. It was exciting to know that our children would only be a couple of months' difference in age and they would grow up together like brothers just as Corey and Courtney had.

Less than a month later, Johnathan Tori Davis was born. It was Nov 7th, 1994 and I was right there in the delivery room holding my sister's hand and praying when he entered the world. Johnathan was not only born on the same date that my daughter Katecia was born, but also at the same hour that she was born. He was a beautiful baby boy and the apple of my sister's eye.

Have you heard the saying "if you fail to plan, you plan to fail" well if you haven't let me be the first to tell you that it's true. When I left Germany, I left without a plan. I assumed I would stay with my mom but things didn't quite work out that way so my grandparents took us in. My cousin Dexter was already temporarily staying there but they still managed to make room for us in their tiny home. My grandmother helped out with spoiling Jeremiah by rocking him to sleep on a pillow every night and loving on him every day. School was already in session in DeWitt so I immediately registered Corey and Tashona. Although Katecia turned 5 on November 7th, her birth date was pass the cutoff date to start kindergarten.

I knew I would have to find a job and other living arrangements pretty quick because the $1000.00 the church sent home with me wasn't going to last very long so I signed up for unemployment and began my job search. Once the unemployment kicked in, I began giving my grandparents money for staying there and helping out any other way that I could. I also started paying on the fines that I left behind in Pine Bluff, i.e. the jeans incident. It took several trips to Pine Bluff with my baby sister riding shotgun, but I finally got them paid off.

Every week I got the Sunday paper and just like an avid fisherman, I threw out the bait. I applied for jobs that I was qualified for and ones that I was not qualified for. I was strong in my faith and was walking in it fully. Finally after a couple of months I got a bite from Southwest Airlines. They were opening a new reservations center in Little Rock that would be located across from the airport. The letter stated that I was selected to be a Reservation Agent and that I would be required to complete 3 weeks of training. I was beyond excited to say the least but just before I could reach elatedness, I read the last few lines of the letter which said, *"the training is unpaid"*—I was drove. Despite all of my efforts, Southwest Airlines had been the only bite that I had gotten so I decided to go ahead and pursue it. I had 99 problems and the lack of transportation was only one. What about the children?

You already know this, but God is so amazing! Two weeks

before my training was to start my car arrived at the port in New Orleans. My brother Keith agreed to drive me there, so the two of us, along with my mom, her acquaintance and Katecia went down to retrieve it. When we got there I found out that the orders showed Solathian as owner of the vehicle which meant his signature would be required before the car could be released to me. The problem was, Solathian was still in Germany.

By God's grace, I somehow made contact with Solathian and explained my situation. He informed me that his mom had power of attorney and could sign on his behalf. He also said he would contact her and have her to meet us in New Orleans the next day. New Orleans was only a few hours' drive from Pensacola so he was sure she would not mind. In order to meet up with Solathian's mom the next day, I got a hotel so that my mom and Katecia could spend the night with me down there and Keith and my mom's acquaintance headed back to Arkansas.

Early the next morning Solathian's mom met us at the hotel with power of attorney to sign papers in Solathian's stead and we all headed to the port. Not only did she come, but Solathian's grandmother and one of his aunts' came along also. They were excited to see Katecia and she was excited to see them. When the paperwork was signed and it was time for us to leave, they wanted Katecia to go back to Florida with them. Although she did not have any clothes with her, they insisted they would buy her everything she needed. I was reluctant at first because Katecia was flat foot showing out. It was only when everyone including her great-grandmother Bill started getting emotional that I agreed to let her go.

My mom and I had a great time catching up during the drive

back home. It took us 6 1/2 hours, but we made it safely back to Arkansas without incident. The next morning during my prayer time I marveled at how God is always on time. I thanked him for meeting not only my transportation need but that He also answered my prayer for someone to watch the children while I went through training. When I got back from New Orleans, my grandmother told me that she would keep the children for me. On top of that, my brother Keith offered to help me out by letting me stay with him and his wife in Little Rock as I went through my training. The plan was for me to stay with them during the week and drive back home on the weekends to be with the children. It would be a little hectic but I knew that I had to do what I needed to do, in order to get in a position to do what I wanted to do.

In my mind all I needed was an ounce of opportunity and a tablespoon of favor because the Lord was with me.

Psalm 118:6

The LORD is on my side; I will not fear:
what can man do unto me?

On My Own

I was very hopeful and excited about starting a new life in Little Rock. Although I knew that there would be challenges, I also knew that God would be with me just as He had when my husband moved out, when I went through 9 months of pregnancy alone and when I had to quit my job due to health complications. Giving up was not an option and I knew I *did not* have the right to remain silent concerning God's goodness under any circumstances.

When my 3 weeks of training were finally over I began working *with pay* at the reservations center. After receiving my first pay check and adding the money I received from unemployment I saved, I was able to find a small 3 bedroom home in Southwest Little Rock that fit into my budget. About a week later my furniture was delivered and I went and got the children from Dewitt. I had invited my sister to move in with me so shortly after the children came she and her baby boy moved in with us.

I really enjoyed working at the airlines but the hours sucked. There had been two classes prior to mine which meant the people from those classes had seniority and first dibs at bidding for the day shifts. Since my shift was an evening to morning shift, my sister stayed with the children at night while I worked and I was there with the babies during the day while she worked. Although it was a challenge at times we made it work. Tupac said "mama made miracles every Thanksgiving" but I say God performed miracles every day including Thanksgiving in our house. The struggle was real!

Everything was going fairly well for the first six months or so and then I blew the head gasket in my car. I guess my days of driving without limits on the Autobahn and not keeping it serviced the way I should have caught up with me. Since my car was our only mode of transportation at the time, we were in trouble.

Keith began helping out in every way he could and then our mom let us use a car that she had. It got us from point A to point B but it had a few issues. Besides needing several coats of paint, it had a radiator leak that required us to put water in it regularly. Since it was winter when we got the car, it also required us to unthaw the water that had frozen in the radiator each morning before we could go anywhere. We did that for a few months and then we got our brother Ed's car. It was a cute little sports car that sat low to the ground. We were able to enjoy it for two or three months before someone saw it, liked it as much as we did and stole it out of the driveway. It was my night off and I had fallen asleep watching T.V. on the couch in the living room. I never heard a thing. I got up the next morning, looked out the window and the car was gone. I woke my sister and she and I stared out the window in disbelief for a few minutes before calling the police. A few days later the police found the car on a back road not far from the house—apparently, very shortly after stealing the car, the culprits ran out of gas.

Although they did some damage to the car, it was still drivable. We had to laugh to keep from crying.

At some point, I realized that being out on my own in that season of my life was actually my opportunity for a redo. I was determined to handle things better and do things better than when I lived in Louisville. I was at a better place in my life and though I was out on my own, I had grown enough in the Lord to know that I wasn't really alone because my Daddy promised in His Word that He would never leave nor forsake me.

I must confess that although I knew in my heart that God was there, there were still times that I allowed the cares of the world to cause me to feel totally absent from His presence.

Deuteronomy 31:6

"Be strong and of a good courage, fear not, nor be afraid of them: for the Lord thy God, he it is that doth go with thee; he will not fail thee nor forsake thee."

Tha' Rock

I never lived, nor hardly ever visited Little Rock in all the years that I had lived in Arkansas. The farthest that I traveled and ever felt comfortable was Pine Bluff. The only times that I recall that we were in Little Rock were for referred dental or doctor appointments. I'd always heard negative things about the capital city even though many of the people from my home town (including my brothers and a couple of cousins) had relocated and did well there. My reason for wanting to move there was simple, I knew that there would be more opportunities for me and my children in Little Rock than in Dewitt.

Before I left Germany, the HBO special *"Gang War: Bangin' in Little Rock"* came out. I recall when word got around that my family and I were headed back to the states, a minister that *"seemed to be a pillar"* (as Paul is quoted as calling them in Galatians 2:9) asked me where in the states would I be relocating; I told him Little Rock. He said "Little Rock! They banging in tha' Rock!" without batting an eye, I replied "God will protect me". He walked away shaking his head. In that moment I knew what Jesus meant when He said to the disciples "O ye of little faith…"

It wasn't long before I realized that Little Rock wasn't as big or as scary as people, including the minister or the HBO special made it out to be. By the time I arrived, the police had already calmed the majority of the gang banging down. Though still filled with its own issues, I found it to be a pretty nice place to live.

Little Rock wasn't that large but yet I was always getting lost. It was a blessing that I lived close to the interstate that took me straight out by the airport where I worked. Finding other destinations proved to be more of a problem but over time I began finding my way.

As for work, I loved my job! When I got there and got on the phones it was so exciting because I was communicating with people that were flying all across the United States. Sometimes I envied their ability to book multiple flights at a time to go where ever they wanted to go, whenever they wanted to go. Many of the flights were for business but most were for pleasure. Although I had free flight benefits, I did not have any money or any place to go.

In the midst of the hustle and bustle of working and taking care of my family, I began missing my husband. He was due to return the following year and would be stationed in Fort Bragg, North Carolina. We had only spoken a few times shortly after I returned to the states and each time it was concerning the children or the child support he was sending. The conversations were always awkward and always short because neither of us really knew what to say. Neither of us apologized to the other for the series of events that led to the demise of our marriage or even discussed our marriage. Although we both were at fault, we secretly blamed each other. Though he never said it, I felt that he still had love for me and our family but that he just loved his freedom more. I could only speculate on his feelings but I did not have to speculate on mine, I was still in love with him.

Though sometimes physically and spiritually exhausted, I knew that I had to keep on pushing and if it were meant for us to get back together God would have to work it out. So much we'd gone through to be together back in 1988/89. Though my heart was still full of love for him, I knew that there was no way that we could be together while on different pages or sides of the world.

While my gut was telling me that I made the right decision by leaving Germany without him, I had to convince myself that I was much more than Solathian's wife and Corey, Jeremiah, Katecia and Tashona's mother. I had not come into the full realization that I was *first* the daughter of *The King* and it was for that reason alone that I deserved more.

I didn't know that not only did I deserve more; God would require more. He wanted me to *"go deeper, further and higher than I'd ever been before"*. The catch was, every ounce of *Tee* would have to die in order for that part of *Twana* to be revealed.

John 12:24

"Verily, verily, I say unto you, except a corn of wheat fall into the ground and die, it abideth alone: but if it die, it bringeth forth much fruit."

Eyes Wide Open

$\mathcal{D}$ays turned into months and months were about to turn into a year when the projected work schedule came out showing that I would finally be on the shift that I had so desperately wanted-the day shift. Southwest was a great company with excellent benefits, but I did not care for their shift bidding process. Although in the beginning I desired the day shift, I realized early on that it was really the night shift that I needed. Despite all my efforts to stay on the night shift, I still ended up on the day shift.

In order to make ends meet, I'd picked up a part time job at a daycare. It was perfect because one of the perks was free childcare for Jeremiah. Not only would day shift bring hardship on me financially (with childcare costs), it would not allow me to keep the second job. I must tell you that it was very hectic working both, but at that time, both were necessary. You see, months prior, my sister was approved for an apartment so she and Johnathan had moved out. When initially accepting the job at Southwest, I did not take the childcare costs or the fact that my sister would eventually get her own place into consideration when accepting the position.

I knew it would be at least a month before the new schedule would go into effect so I began to ponder on ways to keep the job at Southwest. After a couple of days of praying and worrying and worrying and praying, I came up with a plan and the plan would require Solathian's cooperation. That night I sent up prayers asking God to touch his heart.

Solathian was back in the states, stationed in Fort Bragg,

North Carolina. When he first arrived and got settled he joined a church there. He told me that there was a woman there that prophesied to him and said "You and your wife are going to get back together and it will be better than before". Does that sound familiar? If you recall in *"Looking for Love in all the Wrong Places"*, it was the exact same prophecy that had been given to me by a prophetess in Germany right before I left. I had not shared the prophecy with Solathian before, but I shared it with him that day.

Although it would be the only time that we would mention the prophesies, it was the first time in a long time that I felt that there was a little hope for our marriage. I did not fully understand it at the time, but in some instances, you must be totally surrendered to God in order for the prophecy to carry any weight.

Mr. Nuniss had been in the states for several months and had a lot going on. His brother was living with him and money was tight. Money was tight for me too and was about to get tighter if he didn't go along with my plan. I needed him to agree to temporarily let Jeremiah stay with him in North Carolina so that I could give up the part time job at the daycare, keep my job at Southwest and be home with the other children at night. Once I got in a better financial position I would get him back. I figured with his brother being there and not working, he could keep Jeremiah during the day. It took a bit of persuading, but he finally agreed. I used my standby flight privileges, courtesy of Southwest Airlines and flew out to North Carolina a week or so later.

I recall Solathian and his brother being there at the airport waiting on us. He looked at Jeremiah and I could tell that he disapproved of his apparel before the words actually came out of his mouth. He was like "boy we got to go shopping and get you some more clothes." Even though Jeremiah looked like his daddy gave birth to him instead of me, he did not know his daddy. He was only one month old when I left Germany with him. Solathian and I seeing each other for the first time in a long time was awkward, but we made it through it and headed to his apartment.

A neighbor greeted us as we headed into the apartment. SHE was already aware that Jeremiah was coming and went out of her way to speak to him and then to me. I wondered if she knew that I was more than the "baby mama", but instead the wifey. Knowing Solathian a.k.a. Slatewood the way I knew him, I seriously doubted it. The apartment was small and quaint and because my discernment was turned on high, I immediately knew that it was an infamous hangout spot.

Jeremiah was uneasy in his new environment to say the least so he stayed under me practically the entire time. All it took was one night and Solathian realized that he would not be able to keep him because Jeremiah would cry whenever I left the room. The next day he took him shopping and after he got him all dressed up in his new duds, he looked at him and said "Now you look like a Nuniss".

Unfortunately the weekend did not go as I planned and Jeremiah ended up back in tha' Rock with me. I was upset and then I wasn't. I wanted him to stay with his daddy but at the same time I did not feel that the environment was conducive for a child. Knowing how protective I was of my children, I didn't want to take the chance of catching a "charge" so I didn't press the issue.

21

God has a way of redirecting our missteps and getting us back on the right track. I thank Him for that. So many times throughout our separation I desperately wanted to reconcile with Solathian but the trip to North Carolina caused me to pause. That trip caused my eyes to become wide open and see the big picture—the true picture. Solathian had moved on with his life and I had not.

God's can, God's shall and God's will and my can, shall and will were not in direct alignment. Though I traveled back to Little Rock with my son in tow, I knew God had me and eventually He would begin to reveal the plans He had predestined for my life. Something told me that the revelation would come with a price.

Matthew 16:17

"And Jesus answered and said unto him, Blessed art thou, Simon Barjona: for flesh and blood hath not revealed [it] unto thee, but my Father which is in heaven."

My New Normal

My spiritual mind continually reminded me that all things would work together for the good but I promise you that in the natural it did not look like "the good" was going to happen anytime soon.

Mr. and Mrs. Harville, the owners of In His Image Childcare Center (where I worked part time), offered me full time hours and childcare if I came on board with them. It was beneficial for me in one way (no childcare cost) and not as beneficial in other ways (less $$).

Initially it was a hard but I ended up having to say goodbye to Southwest Airlines. Although the daycare was less money, I knew that God was my provider and that I would have to start back walking in that level of faith. While walking this course I found out that the Christian walk can be much more challenging alone than when walking in the company of likeminded people. I was missing your mentorship Karan. ☺

Before leaving Southwest Airlines I did manage to take a trip to my old stomping ground, Louisville Ky. Mama (Grandma Cora) and my Aunt Gwen flew with me using some courtesy passes that I had earned. None of us believed that mama would actually get on the plane but she bravely boarded and sat on the seat between Gwen and me. As we were taking off, she held to the armrest tightly as Gwen and I watched. Once we were in the air, she said "aw, that wasn't that bad". By the time we stopped in St Louis for our layover and took off again she acted like a frequent flyer. Nothing compares to a mother's love; she was going to visit her baby boy, John and older son Charles. We had an awesome time during our stay but when I returned to Arkansas, it was back to business as usual.

Though I saw the strength of my mom and my grandma growing up as a child, I never would have imagined that I would end up having to be the "she-ro" of my family. I believe that it was during this period in my life that I first began to realize how privileged I had been in Germany. The only bills I had there was a car payment and a phone bill. I had a wonderful mentor and a church that I loved. I worked in finance and made good money without having to work hard. I had friends there that were the same friends that I had while stationed in Georgia. Man, those were the days!

Things in Little Rock were a bit harder and a lot lonelier. I could not understand the purpose behind all that I experienced in Germany. Why did I have the encounter with the Holy Spirit? Why did I see and feel the things that I saw and felt? I knew there had to be a purpose for all of it but I did not know what it was. There were many times that I sat and wished that I was back at my grandma's house in the country watching my aunts get dressed to go out on a Saturday night or back when meeting Deb up "on the hill" on a Friday night was the beginning of an awesome weekend.

Being an adult surely was not proving to be as much fun as I thought it would be when I was a little naughty teenager. At 30 years old all I could think was 'mama always told me there would be days like this.

1 Corinthians 13:11
"When I was a child, I spake as a child, I understood as a child, when I became a man I put away childish things"

Life in Pieces

I don't know what made me pick up a newspaper that day but I had been thinking long and hard about moving out of the neighborhood we were living in after Ed's car got stolen. Since the neighborhood was continuing to change more for the worse, I needed a safer haven for my children.

As I combed through the classifieds looking at rentals, I ran across a home that was For Sale by Owner. It was 4 bedrooms, newly remodeled, patio, new appliances, and had a fenced yard. I didn't really have any credit but I knew that if it was meant to be that God would work it out. I stepped out on faith and called the number in the ad and a very nice gentleman answered the phone. The more he told me about the house, the more I wanted it. He gave me the name of someone that worked at a bank and wished me luck. I appreciated his well wishes but I knew that it would take favor and faith to pull it off. Luck was for unbelievers.

I applied for the loan and a few days later, I received a response. Because I did not have much credit and did not make a lot of money, I needed a co-signer. I was disappointed at first but then I decided to step out on faith one more time and ask Solathian to co-sign for me. With reluctance, I dialed his number and told him about the house and the loan situation. Right when I almost lost my nerve, he asked me "What are you going to do". I replied "I need you to cosign". I could tell he was shocked but didn't know which way to answer so instead of saying yes or no, he told me he would think/pray about it. To my surprise after a few days of "thinking it over", he agreed. I could not believe that I was about to become a homeowner. The mortgage would be less than my rent and the house was much nicer. The seller even told me that I would probably end up getting my earnest money back because he was going to pay all my closing costs. On top of that, he called me one day and told me that since the home did not have any trees in the front yard and I had children, he had planted a tree. God had given me favor with this man and I knew it.

I gave my landlord notice and began preparing to box items up to move. I took the children over one day to see the house and they loved it. It seemed like things were finally falling into place for me. My sister and nephew had been gone for a few months and I missed her company very much but I knew that she was on a mission to make things happen for the two of them. She and I were 11 years apart in age, but you could not tell by the level of her maturity. Though we did not always see eye to eye, we always managed to work things out. I had no doubt in my mind that whatever she put her mind to she would accomplish it and she has. We shared many laughs and tears over on Arapaho and through it all I was thankful that my sister was allowed to see God move in my life and hers.

I was on cloud nine anticipating the move into my dream home until that dreaded weekend right before closing. Our time was up at the house I was renting so we'd placed everything in storage. We went to Dewitt that Friday evening and I figured I would get us a hotel for a couple of days when we returned. I was scheduled to close with the title company midweek and then the papers would be overnighted to Solathian for his signature.

I remember being at my dad's house when I got the phone call that changed everything. I don't know why Solathian called me that day but he did. We ended up talking very casually for a few minutes and then somehow an argument ensued. If I am correct it had something to do with child support but I can't be 100% sure about that. Whatever it was, I was heated and he was heated and I made a remark that he would do whatever it was and he declared that he would not. I remember hanging up and as soon as I put the receiver down the picture of the house flashed in my mind. I thought to myself, surely he will not screw up the house deal. He was mad, but I did not think that he was mad enough to do anything like that. I quickly dismissed the thoughts and enjoyed my weekend.

I arrived back in Little Rock early Monday morning, dropped the children off at school and walked into the daycare for work. Mrs. Harville was sitting at her desk like always. I walked in and spoke to her and could tell immediately that something was terribly wrong. She asked me to take a seat and proceeded to tell me that the title company called and said that Solathian had backed out on the deal. He told them that he would not sign the papers to close on the house. In the most sympathetic voice I think I have ever heard, she told me that they also told her that without his signature I did not qualify for the loan. For a moment I sat there in disbelief, then tears began slowly streaming down my face.

Proverbs 15:1
"A soft answer turneth away wrath;
but grievous words stir up anger."

Torn Between Two Lovers

Chapter II

Broke, Busted and Disgusted

Mrs. Harville consoled me as best as she could and then graciously allowed me to go in the back to get myself together. I immediately called the title company and they confirmed everything that Mrs. Harville said. The lady I spoke to told me that if I could get him to change his mind before that upcoming Wednesday we could still close but that he had made it pretty clear to them that it wasn't going to happen.

For the first time in a long time, I felt completely helpless. I did not immediately pray to God. I did not reflect on past trials and how God had brought me through. I only thought of revenge! How dare the man that I had once loved more than my career, my livelihood and seemingly myself, betray me in such a way? I was about to be homeless with 4 kids—two of them his own! I felt the former "Tee" rising up in me and *she* was thinking some real crazy stuff. In *her* mind she could see herself already in North Carolina with a scowl on *her* face, the knife in *her* hand and small hand gun in *her* purse; she was flattening tires and wreaking havoc all over the place. Right when *she* was about to pick up the phone to call and cuss Solathian out and let him know if *she* had to spend every dime *she* didn't have to get to him she would… the Holy Spirit caused **me** to "step back into the light" and **I** came to myself. I realized two very significant things during those moments, #1 that Tee was truly not dead and # 2 that some of the antics that Kav taught me were still fresh in my mind.

It took a little while but I finally regained my composure and dialed Solathian's number. When I heard his voice on the other end I said "Hello" as politely as I could. I did not mince words but got straight to the point. I asked him point blank and period why he backed out. With only a slight hesitation, he began telling me that our conversation over the weekend had left him feeling uncomfortable. He stated that I acted as if he was obligated to help me get the house and that he wasn't. He went on to say that I gave him the impression that he would be the one stuck with the mortgage in the end. When I explained that by backing out on the deal we would be homeless, he did not appear bothered or concerned which really bothered and concerned me. I could not believe that he was being that cold hearted. He had done a lot of messed up stuff in the past and so had I, but never to the point that it impacted the livelihood of our children in such a way.

Despite my assurance that his interpretation of what I said that Saturday was wrong, he still refused to move forward with the deal. The nice 4 bedroom and 2 bath home with the awesome backyard and the tree that the owner had planted just for me was gone! My "American Dream" had turned into a nightmare on Elm Street! I left the daycare that day with shoulders hung, not knowing what my next step would be.

We ended up checking into a hotel that night and after feeding and getting the children in bed, I laid down and cried. When the cry was over, I began to pray and I cried out to my God just as Jesus cried out to Him from the Cross *"Eloi Eloi La ma Sabathoni"* which interpreted means "My God, My God why has thou forsaken me?" For the first time in a long time, I felt completely abandoned by God. Needless to say, I did not get much sleep that night but after many hours of pacing the floor, I was finally able to fall asleep. The next morning the Lord woke me up as if to say *"Talitha Cumi"* which interpreted means *"Daughter arise"*. A new day had begun rather I wanted it to or not. The truth of the matter is that I had to continue to do what I had to do for me and mine. I knew I had no choice but to walk it out—one day at a time. It had been determined from my experiences early in life that time does not wait for you to get yourself together before it moves on.

I must say it was the grace of God that kept us during our 2 1/2 month stay in the hotel. I wasn't making much money but I was able to pay the hotel bill each week and buy gas and food. While there I recall hurting my foot while sitting out by the pool one day. I got up to get something and somehow my foot twisted and I fell. I thought it was minor but it ended up being sprained and caused me to walk with a limp for almost a week or so. I was being kicked while I was already down but God's anointing was still on me and I was able to take a licking and keep on ticking.

We had a weekly routine of driving down home on Friday evenings, staying at my dad's house and driving back on Monday mornings. I'd drop the three oldest children off at school and would take the baby to daycare with me. The routine was etched in my children's brains so that even baby Jeremiah, who was 2 at the time, would fall right into his car seat on Friday evenings ready for the ride. Although we were becoming more bonded as a family, at times I felt hopeless and wanted to scream to the top of my lungs "I can't do this anymore!!!!!" Every time I felt that way, I would get my cry on, the Holy Spirit would comfort me, and I would regain the strength I needed to face another day.

I thank God for Mr. and Mrs. Harville, who were not only my bosses, they were also ministers and I learned a lot from them. Mrs. Harville prayed for me and shared testimonies of how God had blessed them over the years. She was and still is the best storyteller ever. With her soft voice and meek demeanor, she would have you hanging on to the edge of your seat, anxious to see what she would say next. Mr. Harville was not only a great spiritual father but a great leader. It always put a smile on my face when I heard Mrs. Harville call him "honey". (Rest in love Mr. Harville)

As great as they were, not even Mrs. Harville's awesome stories were able to keep me from heading into the dark place I was going spiritually. I was trying to figure out how to get us out of the hotel and was becoming very discouraged. The money was not adding up—as soon as I made it, I had to spend it. It felt like the weight of the world was all on my shoulders.

It wasn't long before I began to question my spirituality, my mentality and my purpose. My life was not the fairy tale life that I once wrote about and certainly nowhere near what I dreamed of as a child. The cards I was dealt resembled a real bad spades hand-a whole lot of hearts and not one spade to be found.

Matthew 11:28, 29

Come unto me all ye that labor and are heavy laden, and I will give you rest. Take my yoke upon you and learn of me for I am meek and lowly in heart and you will find rest unto your souls, for my yoke is easy and my burdens are light.

$\mathcal{A}$ Brilliant Disguise

$\mathcal{T}$hings did not get better but instead got worse although no one on the outside looking in could tell. Solathian and I were still at odds and began talking about getting a divorce *again*. Several months before moving out of the house on Arapaho and before I attempted to buy the house, the subject of divorce had come up, but neither of us wanted to be the first one to file. If you recall, Solathian got saved in Heidleberg as well so he was aware of what the bible said about divorce. We had been married 7 long years and all of the fight was out of me. Seven was the number of completion and we were both finding ourselves wanting to be *completely* done with the other.

After the subject of divorce first came up, I spoke to a couple of lawyers that basically told me the same thing. Because Solathian was military and he made decent money, I could get as much as $400 per child from him in child support and spousal support as well. My God, however told me that if he filed I was not to contest the divorce or fight him for more money. I was to continue to accept the amount he was sending me because it would end up working out in my favor.

All of the odds were against me in the natural when I left Heidelberg in 1994 with 4 children but I knew that my God was greater than any odds odds because He said in His Word that it was *His* counsel that would stand. I must admit the thought of divorce not only shook me, but caused my faith to waiver tremendously. After all, not just one but two prophets had declared that we would get back together.

I had to smile and keep up a front so that no one would know how broken I was inside. I often thought of Karan and the rest of the ladies that I had grown with in the Lord. I missed our fasting and prayer sessions and the bible studies that were taught by Pastor Fitzgerald. If I were to never see a miracle again, I knew that I saw them while living in Germany. When we prayed things manifested and manifested quickly. I needed Karan to pray me through like she had so many times in the Germany when things in my life were not going right. Instead she and every other crutch that I formerly had was hundreds, some thousands of miles away. God knew what He placed in me and He wanted me to experience Him in a way that I never experienced Him before—completely one on one.

Although I was back *home*, it was not home the way I felt home to be when I was with my church family if that makes sense. I was at a place where I understood what Jesus meant when he asked his disciples, *"Who is my mother? And who are my brethren? And he stretched forth his hand toward his disciples, and said, Behold my mother and my brethren!"* in Matthew 12:48-49.

Day after day I felt myself beginning to weaken more and more spiritually. Rather than drawing closer to God I did the opposite. I began to read my bible less and watch T.V. more. Hour long prayer sessions became 15 minute prayer sessions and my weekly fasting ceased. I was spiritually dying and yet no one ever recognized that I was even sick.

Mark 4:4

"…and it came to pass, as he sowed, some fell by the wayside and the fowls of the air came and devoured it up…"

$\mathcal{A}$ Thin Line between Love and Hate

"...the sweetest woman in the world can become the meanest woman in the world if you make her that way"

$\mathcal{T}$he lyrics from the 1990's song "A Thin Line Between Love and Hate" were proving to be true. Solathian informed me that he had finally started the process of filing for divorce. Even though I had literally began to hate him in my heart, we still had to communicate at times regarding the children. Not only was I bitter about the house incident, but I was also bitter about him continuing to mention filing for divorce. My heart had become hardened and I began to see a side of myself that I thought no longer existed.

I remember when I first arrived in Little Rock I was so on fire for God. I wanted to evangelize and do all of the things that I had not been able to do while in Germany like feeding the homeless and walking the streets sharing the gospel. I recall telling my brother Ed that I wanted to go to "The Pines" to evangelize and he told me that the apartments had a bad reputation and that I may want to reconsider. I told him I wasn't afraid because I was *covered by the blood of Jesus* and he jokingly replied "you going to be covered *in* blood if you go messing around in The Pines." Needless to say, I didn't go to The Pines.

For weeks I searched the newspaper for houses and apartments that would fit into my tight budget, but finally had to settle on the infamous Pines Apartments; the apartments my brother warned me about. The Harville's graciously offered to pay the first month's rent if I covered the utilities and security deposit. I somehow came up with the money and scheduled an appointment to view the inside.

As soon as I toured the complex with the leasing agent and looked at the apartment that we would be living in, I knew that it was going to be a challenge. The apartments were not well-kept and still had one of the worst reputations in Southwest Little Rock just like my brother said. The Pines were most infamously known for it's alleged drug activity. Many also felt that most of the tenants that lived there were on welfare and didn't want anything out of life. This was true in some cases but of course not all, as I was a witness. People warned me of kids running amuck, women sitting around all day doing (styling) hair, smoking weed, and talking about what they did at the club. It was also said that there would be a lot of "no good" men standing around drinking, selling weed and playing cards all day instead of working.

There was only one way in and out of The Pines, the front gates. Although there were gates, there was no security. It did not require a key card or code to enter because they were left open both day and night which didn't make any sense to me. I got my furniture out of storage on a Saturday and prepared to move in the first floor apartment that had been assigned to us. Not only was I in The Pines, our apartment was in back of the complex.

As we drove through the gates in the U-Haul truck that Saturday there were people sitting out on their balconies and porches checking us out. There were children running (amuck) around buildings and playing in yards. I could hear music coming out of some of the apartments and guys hung out on the side of buildings (selling weed and playing cards) and a couple of ladies were sitting out on their balcony (talking loud and doing hair). I saw immediately that there was indeed plenty of evangelistic work that could have been done at The Pines.

Although I had seen a lot and learned a lot while under the leadership of Pastor Fitzgerald and Karan, evangelizing not only required dedication to God, it required wisdom. Though once zealous, part of my fire had been extinguished therefore as we rode through The Pines on moving day I wasn't thinking about evangelizing. I was trying to figure out how I was going to keep my children safe.

As we slowly passed through the complex, I wondered–is there some type of escape route? Why is trash on the ground every place I look? Why is that woman staring at me? Where did he come from? How did they get over that fence? Whose kids are those and why are they playing in those dumpsters? Is that weed I'm smelling? If so, what kind? I was completely in the natural— NO spiritual thoughts were entering my mind.

We unpacked the truck, settled in for bed and before the last light went out, I heard a single gunshot. It wasn't New Year's so I could only assume it was the way they said "welcome" to the new tenants. Jeeeeeesuuuuussss!!! I got on my knees, thanked God that we were no longer in a hotel and asked him to encamp His angels around to protect us.

Little did I know that the devil had me right where he wanted me. I wasn't praying like I used to. I wasn't fasting like I used to. I did not have a covering (a church home). I wasn't putting on my armor and I was not studying the Word. I had stepped into the devil's territory spiritually naked and unarmed.

While I was focusing on my living situation and pending divorce, the devil had gone before God requesting that he remove the hedge that He had around me. I didn't know it, but God granted his request with only one condition—you can't have her life.

Isaiah 54:7, 8

"For a mere moment I have forsaken you, but with great mercies I will gather you. With a little wrath I hid my face from you for a moment; but with everlasting kindness I will have mercy on you" Says the Lord, your Redeemer.

*F*ive Miles to Empty

*I*t did not take long after moving into The Pines, which I nicknamed "The Jungle", that I knew that I would have to step up my praying game in order to survive. I began to ask God to encamp angels around our apartment and around the complex religiously. I was binding demonic spirits in Jesus name and loosing peace and protection over the roach infested apartment we called home. It was a day to day thing—a do or die thing. It was an honor to wake up without a burglar staring me in the face, some stranger crawling through my window and not being awakened by the ringing of gunshots. When I found all 4 of my children neatly tucked in their beds each morning I considered myself blessed. We had lived to *live* another day. Ed's words stuck in my head and kept me on edge for a while but after being there a few months I found that it was not quite as bad as I thought or maybe we just began to fit in.

Working at the daycare was my refuge. I began to pour myself into the ministry that God had spoken to me a couple years prior, *"The 12 Months of Christmas™"*. Through that program I began to collect donations of toys, clothing and food to distribute to the less fortunate. I began to work with the youth in the afterschool program at the center also. Just when I seemed to have gotten my second wind "them" papers came. (I just call them "them" because they destroy lives and are evil).

I cannot express in words the feeling that I felt when I received "them". There was a hollowness in my soul and I felt sick, both physically and spiritually. It was a feeling that you feel when someone you love so dearly dies. In essence it was a death, the death of a covenant that was not only made between the two of us, but one that we made to God.

I still loved/hated Solathian prior to receiving "them". My emotions were all over the place as I tried to figure out if I would do what God said and not contest the divorce or do what Tee wanted to do and take him to the cleaners. Very quickly my love began to move further into the background and my hate moved closer to the forefront. You see, prior to him backing out on the house and filing for divorce I had secretly hoped for a reconciliation. Despite how dirty he'd been at times, I still wanted the prophecy to be true that the two women prophesied. It would be years later before I would learn that prophecy is conditional and that if we do not receive and protect the prophecy that we can *delay* it from coming to pass but cannot *deny* it from coming to pass if it is truly of God.

I decided to go the high road and follow God's instructions; this in turn caused things to work out in my favor. By not contesting and asking for more child support or spousal support, Solathian began sending the children and me extra money. It was a gracious effort but just as money can't buy you love, it can't buy you forgiveness either.

When everything seems to be going left, God will step in and make things right. In my case He sent a young man to the daycare that we called "Brother T". Brother T was a student of the Word and a bonafide prophet. He and his family had moved to Little Rock from Southern Arkansas. He was in need of a job so the Harville's hired him to work at the center. He helped out with administration and he also picked up children after school and brought them to the center. I was so excited to have someone to expound with on the Word. He and I would talk about the Word of God all throughout the day and encourage each other in the faith. He was one of the first true Prophet's that I had met since coming to Little Rock, the other being Apostle Lawrence Braggs.

Brother T and I were both searching for the same thing, a church where the Word of God was being preached uncompromisingly and where signs and wonders were following. Needless to say, neither of us had found such a place. I was thankful for a big brother in Christ that was able to challenge my thinking and challenge me in growing in the Word because in actuality, I was still a babe in Christ. Although I had tasted meat, I was far from being perfected (mature) in my walk with God. He challenged my thinking and I challenged his. He was like the big spiritual brother that I never had.

Brother T separated from his wife not long after starting to work at the center and for a brief moment the enemy tried to cause us to see each other in another way; a romantic way. It wasn't that we were truly attracted to each other, we were just both in vulnerable states and the devil knew that. I was recently divorced at the time and he was separated from his wife. I thank God that we were able to combat it and our friendship remained intact. He and his wife eventually reconciled and moved back to Southern Arkansas.

It was around January 1997 and Lord knows that I had been through a lot. The only thing that was bringing me joy was my children and my job. I did not have any idea that my time at the center was about to end until one day as I was finishing up some

TORN BETWEEN TWO LOVERS

paperwork I heard the Lord telling me so clearly that it was time to put in my two-week notice. When He spoke to me I answered Him by saying to myself, "I have 4 children at home and bills" as if He didn't already know that. The prompting in my spirit was so intense that I could not ignore it so I sat there and began to write out my two week notice.

Before leaving that evening I reluctantly handed the notice to Mrs. Harville. When I put it in her hand she looked as puzzled as I had felt when God told me to do it. All I could tell her was that God said so.

I remember my brother, Mr. "You going to be covered in blood" coming by my apartment that evening. He knew the Harvilles because he did some carpentry work for them from time to time. I told him that I put in my notice and he asked me "well what are you going to do now?" I simply answered "trust God". Since my friend, Brother T, had moved on I didn't have anyone to confer with or turn to for advice. I had lost contact with Karan and had not talked to her in years. I had to totally trust in the fact that I heard correctly.

While sitting at home trying to figure out what God was doing, I recalled a storefront church that Brother T had discovered and took me to. It was called *"Led by the Spirit of God Church"*. It was a small family church and the Spirit of God was really moving the Sunday that we went. I liked the atmosphere but I knew I could not join any church without knowing 100% that it was God leading me there. Of the many churches I visited, Led by the Spirit was definitely at the top of my list. I thought of visiting again to see if God would give me more clarity on why He had me to put in my notice. Foolishly, I disregarded the thought almost as quickly as it came to mind but vowed to myself to visit Led by The Spirit again one day.

Intuition is another way that God speaks to us. I could have saved myself a whole lot of trouble if I had acted upon my first thought.

Proverbs 3:5-6

"Trust in the Lord with all thine heart; and lean not unto thine own understanding. In all thy ways acknowledge Him, and He shall direct thy path."

Deja' Vu

I was searching the newspaper for another job when I ran across an ad for positions at a new hospital that was about to open, called *The Arkansas Heart Hospital.* They had a position in the finance dept. and since I worked as a Payroll Technician in Germany, I decided to apply for it and a few other accounting jobs. Though nervous at times, I continued to stand in my faith that I heard God. At the end of my two weeks at the daycare center my standing in faith paid off. I received a call for an interview at the Heart Hospital and a week later I landed the job. The new job not only meant more money, but an opportunity for a career in a field that I enjoyed. I had a couple of weeks before I would begin working at the hospital so I began to prepare myself. Things were finally looking up.

Everything I needed was within walking distance of the jungle so I would often walk to get groceries or whatever. One day as I was walking from Walgreens, headed to my apartment, I was stopped by a gentleman in a red car. After staring me up and down for a couple of seconds he asked me for my name. He was looking kind of crazy so I figured I better tell him something. I hesitantly gave him the name of my alter ego—Tee. He told me that his name was *Lee. He wasn't the most handsome guy but not the worst looking guy I had seen either. He was old school, though not that old. After talking for a few minutes I found him to be funny and kind of charming. He asked for my number and when I declined he told me that he had friends in the complex and that he would run into me again. As he drove off I smiled to myself feeling somewhat flattered. It had been years since someone had actually tried to come at me in that manner. I had a couple of brief conversations in the past with a friend of my sister's boyfriend named *Joe but nothing transpired. One day Joe caught me in the middle of watching a T.D. Jake's sermon and I did not allow anyone to come between me and a good T. D. Jakes sermon so that was the end of him.

When I wasn't working I stayed in my house with my children and minded my business. The only time I was out of the house was when I went shopping, to the children's schools or down to the country. My sister Sharonica was my bestie and her home was the hangout spot when I just wanted to watch a movie in peace or have some girl talk. Although I had not found me a permanent church home I would attend the Lighthouse Church which was pastored by Mr. and Mrs. Harville occasionally. I tried my best to be faithful but my visits to church during that time were far and in between. Due to my lack of dedication at the church, I quickly found out that an idle mind really is the devil's workshop. One day while sitting and daydreaming, I started thinking about that complete stranger—Lee. Although we had only spoken briefly his words seemed to have watered a root that was still inside of me. F.Y.I. If you don't destroy a thing at the root —it *will* come back.

In relation to the trap that had been set, I ran into Lee again. This time he was with one of his little homeboys. The homeboy wore a dangling earring in one ear that my sister and I grew to hate. This time he told me that he wanted to get to know me better etc., and that one of his friends in the complex was having a barbeque the upcoming Saturday and he wanted me to go as his guest. He was more talkative than he had been in the past so I accounted that to the beer that he had in his hand. He went on to share with me that he was single and had a son and that he and his son's mother were not together. He spoke of his sisters and wanted me to meet them. He asked for my number again and again I declined. Although I enjoyed Lee's conversation, I was not trying to jump into a relationship with anyone that quickly. I had been there and done that.

When I got saved I vowed to myself that the life I once lived was behind me and I was "NEVER" going back! Nunca decir Nunca—Never say never….

Mark 4:5

"…and some fell on stony ground , where it had not much earth and immediately it sprang up, because it had no depth of earth. But when the sun was up it was scorched, and because it had not root, it withered away…"

$\mathcal{H}$ow Low *Will You Go?*

I finally began my new job at the Heart Hospital. Since all of us were new employees, training to become an Accounts Payable Specialist was so much easier. Although the hospital signed my checks, I actually worked for Marriott. Mariott had a contract with the hospital to provide all of their food and environmental services. I shared a small office with my supervisor, Colleen, who was very cool. She had transferred from another Heart Hospital out west in order to get Arkansas' up and running.

At times while on my way to work or when I was returning home from work, I would see Lee. Sometimes he would wave as I passed by and other times he would stop me and we would talk. Finally one day when he stopped me and after asking me for my number for the 100th time, I reluctantly gave it to him. Something was telling me not to do it, but just as before, I ignored it. The phone calls began and I quickly felt myself slipping. I knew almost immediately that I was slowly transforming back into "Tee" because whenever I was around Lee, even my mannerisms were different.

I introduced my sister to Lee and his friends and she began hanging out over in the jungle with me. There was always drinking and partying at one of his homeboy's girlfriends' apartment (They were what TLC referred to as "Scrubs"). There was always lots of food and drinks but when my sis and I saw fly traps full of flies hanging all around at this one apartment, we passed on the food. We were completely entertained by just watching all the interesting looking people that were there.

Lee eventually introduced me to his younger sister and I clicked with her immediately. Before long she began to hang out at my apartment and I met other members of their family through her. There were always barbecues and gatherings but no one was gathering at the church. Well let me rephrase that, I wasn't involved in any gatherings that included people the group of people I was hanging out with at a church.

Before long and without realizing it, I had allowed myself to slip right out of the arms of God and back into the world. It happened so quickly that I didn't see it coming. By the time that I realized where I was, I woke up early one morning in the arms of Lee. I cannot adequately describe the guilt and shame that I felt as I slid from the bed that morning and gathered my things. Not only had I let God down, I had let myself down. I had opened myself up to be back in the same situation that I had been in so many years before. The only difference was that I was not *looking for love*—my heart was still too numb from my failed marriage for that. I had merely allowed the enemy to infiltrate my life through the spirit of loneliness. The devil doesn't have any new tricks—he doesn't need any because we still fall for the old ones.

By not staying in my Word and by not staying in God's face I became vulnerable. I had not recalled to mind the words that my mentor had spoken to me before I left Gemany. She said, *"You are a woman of God and God will use you mightily, stay strong"*. When you don't realize your purpose, you can't live *on* purpose. I did not think that there was any way that God could use me after falling back into sin. I did not realize that God knew where I would end up before I got there.

The prodigal son left his father's house thinking he was mature enough to make it on his own. Just like the prodigal son, I too was about to experience what it felt like to leave the protective arms of your father and then find yourself covered in pig manure.

Proverbs 10:9

"He that walketh uprightly, walketh surely; but he that perverteth his ways shall be made known."

Journey of the
Prodigal Daughter

The following weekends were spent doing things just like back in the day. I was hanging around people that were drinking and smoking and hanging out at parties. I was also involved in a sexual relationship with Lee. I recall the first weeks of our relationship were filled with guilt but the more that I hung out, the easier it became. The flesh is like that, it can adapt to things pretty easily.

Although I had accepted God as my Lord and Savior, my heart had not been fully changed nor had my mind been fully renewed—there was no way that it could have been. God is Holy and they that worship Him must do so in Spirit and in truth. There are just some things we should not be able to do because of our deep love and fear (reverence) of God.

Although I was "out there" in every sense of the word, I would still stop every once in a while and send up a (ritual, religious, scribes and Pharisees type) prayer or two to God. Most of those times were when times were tough and a bill was past due or I didn't have gas in the car or whatever. I was not praying for the sake of giving God his due praise. I was praying out of my flesh, begging God to help me in spite of my wretched lifestyle. As soon as the need was met, the realization of his blessing quickly rested far in the back of my mind.

It wasn't long before Lee and I began to have problems. I would stop talking to him and then start back. Stop talking to him again and start back again. Inspite of what he and I went through, I remained cool with his sisters and one of them (the oldest) smoked "Mary Jane". Well you know that was my vice back in the day so it wasn't long before I began smoking too. The first time I hit it, I was taken aback because it had been so long since I had smoked but as soon as "it" kicked in, I realized how much I had missed her. Not only did his sister begin to invite me over to smoke, I began getting my own from one of her sources to take to her house to smoke. Though it wasn't an everyday thing, it was more often than it should have been. If it had not been for my job I'm sure it could have quickly turned into an everyday thing. Even though I was acting crazy, I wasn't completely crazy. I loved my job and could not afford to lose it for Mary Jane or anyone else so after a while I completely stepped back from smoking.

Lee never tried to move in with me and only spent the night a couple of times. I also began to see him less than I had in the beginning which were both clues that there was another woman. Then one day as if a huge light bulb went off in my head and scales fell from my eyes, I began to see the real Lee. The lying, cheating, lazy, don't really have a job, don't have a relationship with God and still in a relationship with his baby mama Lee! The Lee that had merely been broken up with his baby mama when I first met him and the Lee whose baby's mama found out about me and began calling and harassing me. The baby mama that when I was dropping him off one night threw a brick and hit my car and was given the nickname of "Ernest T Bass" by my brother Ed. (For those who do not know "Ernest T" was the rock yielding town drunk on *The Andy Griffith Show*).

Lee wasn't one for drama so when I told him it was over,

he did not put up a fuss but instead 'fessed up. He told me that although he and his son's mother were having problems, he loved his son and wanted to be with him. I couldn't do anything but respect that despite the circumstances so we parted ways.

In the midst of me trying to get out of the mess I had gotten myself into, an amazing thing happened. After being in the jungle for only about 9 months I got approved for a home loan.

There had been a home advertised in the paper for rent so I called about it and the agent agreed to show it to me the following day after I got off work. When we first entered the house, I noticed that it wasn't much better than the roach infested apartment that we were already living in so I declined. As we were leaving the agent asked me if I had considered purchasing a home. I explained to her that I had applied before and had needed a co-signer and how all of that had ended with my ex backing out. She reassured me that since I was making more money at my new job I would probably qualify by myself. She told me that she had a listing that she thought that I would like and could show it to me after I went to the lender and applied for a loan.

My two oldest were teenagers and were running a "mild" wild like the rest of the teenagers in the jungle and my two youngest weren't far behind them. They knew I didn't play so they were very discreet; still I knew that I needed to get them out of the jungle.

A few days after applying, I got the news that I was approved for the loan without needing a cosigner so the agent showed me one of her listings. It was a beautiful 3-bedroom house in a cul de sac, with a den, a huge kitchen and it was sitting on almost a half-acre of land. It was located near an elementary school and was convenient to my job. We all loved it so much that on June 1st, 1997, I walked out of the title company with the keys in my hand. Although Lee and I were not seeing each other, he agreed to get a couple of his homeboys to help me move from the jungle into my new house. Big mistake!

The thought did not occur to me that *a house that is not built on a firm foundation would not be able to stand* or that *unless God builds the house, he that labors, labors in vain.* Instead my mind went more towards the lyrics from Luther Vandross song, *A House is not a Home.* I especially loved the part that that says.... *"a room is still a room even when there's nothing there but gloom, but a room is not a house, and a house is not a home, when the two of us are far apart and one of us has a broken heart"...*

Circumstantially, it wasn't Lee that I was thinking about either. Sang Luther! You better Sang!!

James 4:4
"Ye adulterers and adulteresses, know ye not that the friendship of the world is enmity with God? whosoever therefore will be a friend of the world is the enemy of God."

55

M oving on Up!!

I was so excited to have realized the American Dream of homeownership and everyone loved it. Even Solathian was surprised when I told him I had bought a house. It had not been long before that I needed his signature to get a home and although he backed out on that one—God gave me another one, or so I thought. If you know what I know, you will agree that the devil will give you stuff when you serve him too.

The children were so excited to have a new home. Corey had his own room, the girls shared a room and Jeremiah would sleep with me. Eventually, Corey got booted from his own room for one reason or another and would sleep in the den. It was a little tight having 4 kids and only 3 bedrooms but Corey did not seem to mind sleeping in the den when he was there. It crossed my mind that it may have been because there was a door that led outside. I'm almost 100% positive he was using it. Overall our new place was a mansion in comparison to the hotel room and the roach motel in "the jungle".

Shortly after getting the house, my car got hit so I ended up having to get another one. Even though I needed the car, it was an unwelcomed expense. The job afforded me the ability to maintain but things were beginning to get tight. I loved my new home but it was proving to be a lot more expensive than the apartment or the hotel. Although I was making decent pay, I knew that in order to advance and get more pay, I would need some additional education. I did some research on colleges and began taking classes part time at Pulaski Technical College in

North Little Rock. My hope was to receive my accounting degree and a pay raise.

Out of the blue, Lee called me one day and told me that he and his girl broke up… again. As you probably predicted, it wasn't long before we began messing around… again, though short-lived. I learned a valuable lesson while messing around with Lee. When a person shows you who they are, you are supposed to believe them. The final straw for Lee and I came courtesy of "Ernest T".

One night while he and his younger sister were over visiting, this familiar looking car goes flying by my house. It was the same car that Lee was in the very first time I met him. Since I lived in a cul de sac, the car had no choice but to turn around and come back. It was Lee's baby mama, a.k.a. "Ernest T". I later found out that one of his homeboys, the one that wore the dangling earring that drove my sister and me crazy, gave her my address. He was also one of the guys that helped Lee move me in my house. Lee went out and talked to her and a few minutes later she went spinning off. I noticed by the brake lights that it was also the car that she had thrown the brick out of that night I dropped him off at his sister's house.

Lee and I had a long talk that night and decided to part ways. It was obvious that even if she didn't want him as he proclaimed, she didn't want him with me. I was not about to have *"Ernest T"* breaking the windows out of my car or house so Lee and I parted ways for good. Although I did not believe that my encounter with Lee could replace the call that was on my life or the love that God *still* had for me, I could not seem to find my way back home.

When I reflect back, I honestly don't believe that I truly had a desire to go back home at that time. Strangely enough it all began to make sense when I received the revelation that the monster I had awakened inside of me, was not ready to be put back to bed.

Luke 11: 24-26

"When the unclean spirit is gone out of a man, he walketh through dry places, seeking rest; and finding none, he saith, I will return unto my house whence I came out. And when he cometh, he findeth it swept and garnished. Then goeth he, and taketh to him seven other spirits more wicked than himself; and they enter in, and dwell there: and the last state of that man is worse than the first."

Torn Between Two Lovers

Chapter III

$\mathcal{D}$ivine Interruption

$\mathcal{W}$hen I got the phone call I was in shock! My 16-year-old son was about to be a father? At 33 years old I was about to be somebody's *grandma?*

We had not been in our new home but about 3 or 4 months when I received the news. The young lady lived in 'the jungle" and had gotten pregnant by my firstborn prior to us leaving there. I had been too busy trying to get my groove on to realize that Corey was out getting his on as well. The young lady's mother, Ms. S.* called me and we scheduled a date and time to meet up and discuss the situation. I had already decided that if the young lady did not want the child that we would have to step up and do what we had to do. Because of my personal experience with abortion, I knew that there was no way that I was going to allow that notion to be put on the table. Personally, it was the one thing out of all of the bad things I had done in my life that had haunted me the longest and that I found the hardest to forgive myself for.

I sympathized with the young lady's mother because I knew it must have been hard to see her baby getting ready to have a baby at such a young age. I also sympathized with the young lady because I knew firsthand the obstacles that she would face as a teenage mother. Though the facts (statistics) say children born to teenage mothers are more likely to "have lower school achievement and drop out of high school, give birth as a teen, be incarcerated at some time during adolescence and be unemployed and underemployed as a young adult" The *Truth* says "His Way is perfect, His Word is tried and He is a buckler to all who trust in

Him." In other words, God does not make mistakes. I believed in my heart that my grandchild would beat the odds.

Ms. S. was really cool and I assured her that I would help out with the baby as much as I was able to. Though it cramped our style, being as young and fly as we both were to be grandmas, we agreed that the child didn't ask to come into the world and should not have to suffer.

Corey never denied that the child was his but instead manned up and took responsibility. I admired his sensitivity to the situation considering the fact that his father had not been in his life. It always bothered me that he never really had anyone to pour into him the way that a father should so I often tried to compensate by letting him hang out with me. Although Solathian was my husband and respected and took good care of both Tashona and Corey, at that time in his life he was not there for them in an emotional sense. Since I cannot judge where he was, I just thank God that is *He* is a *Father* to those that are fatherless.

It was March 5th, 1998—my Uncle John's birthday. Corey was 17 years old and the young lady was a few years younger when they became parents and I became the proud "Nana" to Tionna Latrice Joyner. I remember getting the phone call and rushing to the hospital to see her. It was love at first sight; she was such a beautiful baby. Watching Corey hold her for the first time and seeing the way he looked into her eyes made me proud. It was in that moment that I realized that *my baby* had become a man.

Psalm 127:3
*"Lo, children are an heritage of the Lord;
and the fruit of the womb is His reward."*

SPECIAL NOTE: At the time of this writing, Tionna is 18 years old, does not have any children, has purchased 2 cars on her Waffle House salary, has her own apartment and attends Philander Smith College in Little Rock where she is majoring in Math. Talk about beating the odds! If you don't remember anything else I have said, remember this, What God ordains—**He shall maintain!!! Love you Tionna!**

Familiar Spirits

As Corey became a man, his mother was acting less than the Christian lady that she was and should have been. As if I hadn't learned enough lessons from messing around with Lee. About 8 or 9 months after our relationship ended and while out grocery shopping, I met this guy named James*. I caught him watching me while I was in the checkout line and as I exited the building he was standing there. As I began to walk pass him, he flashed me the most handsome smile that I had ever seen and introduced himself as he walked me to my car. As we walked, he told me he was from Helena and was in the city visiting friends. We exchanged phone numbers and though he said he would call me the following day, I wasn't holding my breath. He was just my type—a little rough around the edges and milk chocolate. I was sure that was the line that he fed all the ladies and because he was so F-I-N-E, he could get away with it! I can't lie he was fine! If at first he does not succeed, the devil will try, try again until he sends you what you *really* want.

I was shocked when he actually did what he said he was going to do. He called the next day and we talked for hours. After talking over the phone a couple of weeks, I allowed him to come visit me at my home. Although we had good conversation and chemistry, I did not trust him or a long distance relationship. According to him, he once made a lot of money as a drug dealer in Detroit but lost it and his freedom after being set up by his girlfriend who was also from Helena. Immediately I had a flashback of Kav.

Lord knows Kav had given me a large enough glimpse of thug living and left enough battle wounds for me to know that I no longer wanted to be *'bout that life.* Although James shared his deep dark secrets and assured me that he was no longer in the game, I knew that I did not want to get too close to him. I also wondered why the guys I was meeting was confessing all their business to me as if I was a psychologist or something. Later on in my life it became apparent that it wasn't me but the anointing making them speak.

James tried everything he could to gain my trust. When he was in Helena he would often call and check on me and seemed genuinely concerned about my well-being. Still I could not get into him the way he appeared to be into me. When he was at my house, the den was our favorite place because we were both big movie buffs. When he came down on weekends we would watch movies all night. He made me laugh and was very romantic. He had a thug look but gentleman manners—I call it swag. The chemistry was there but all I could hear in the back of my head was "fool me once, shame on you, fool me twice shame on me", he could blame Lee for that one.

Things for me began to wan out pretty quickly. I began to find him rather needy which I accounted to the fact that he was a mama's boy. He tried to fix us but there was nothing for him to fix. I just wasn't digging him the way that he wanted me to. A period followed when I didn't see him for a couple of weeks and then out of the blue he and a friend showed up on my doorsteps on a weeknight. He generally didn't bring strangers to my house nor did he make it a practice of coming to see me during my workweek. The three us sat in the den and ate chicken wings and began watching a movie. Since I had to go to work the following day, I told him they could finish watching but I was going to bed and to lock the door when he left. I was in bed, but I hadn't fallen asleep and was lying with my face towards the wall when I felt someone get in the bed. I automatically thought it was him coming to get a good bye kiss or to say good-bye or whatever but instead it was his homeboy! I jumped up and every curse word I thought I had forgotten began to flow from my mouth. Were we in high school? Was I some trick they thought they could push up on? Needless to say, that train never left the station and I gave him and the homeboy a heave ho back to Helena. A few weeks later I saw one of his friends that lived locally. He was always very respectful and when he saw me he just started shaking his head. He started by telling me that James told him what happened that night. James said he was digging me and all but that I kept trying to throw him away so when his homeboy told him that I was implying that I wanted *them* to join me in bed that night, he sent him first to see if that was really what I had in mind. James also told him he had never heard me curse before that night but that I cursed him and his homeboy out. He blamed it on being "on one" (slang for high) for going along with it and felt bad but was afraid to call and apologize. Needless to say, that was the end of James. #byejames

My track record since I had returned to the states had proven to be poor; I was 0-3 with neither of the relationships lasting consistently over 4 to 5 months. Before I go any further, let me backtrack to Will* who I met prior to meeting James and right after Lee. He played basketball for an independent team and I believe that is where I first met him. He had a great sense of humor and somewhere along the way we ran into each other again. As my ill-fated journey would have it, he would become another thorn in my side and another fork in my crooked road.

Will and I had a relationship of convenience. Since we had such dynamic chemistry, our times spent together were most often mere hook-up sessions. It was with him that I began to smoke weed again. He always had an ample supply so we would go out in my backyard and get wasted. I loved to laugh and he could make me do that at the drop of a hat. During that time pagers were still being used but we were also in the beginning stages of using those expensive cell phones that looked like house phones. For those of you that can remember the pager, you know in order for the person to know who you were, they entered a secret number code at the end. Mine was #34, which was my age at the time. As we began to get more intimate and into each other, I guess either his conscience or his inability to keep up with his lies got the best of him because he finally shared with me that he was married. As with all cheating liars and the cheating liars they are cheating and lying with, he told me that they were divorcing. I did not believe him, but was enjoying the "hook-up sessions" so I continued to see him.

I believe that it was around this time that I first began to question if anything that I had experienced in Germany was real. I didn't understand fully that though my soul got saved, my nasty flesh did not. I was out of the world, but the world *was not out of me*. When the flesh is left unchecked for a period of time it resorts back to its old ways and mine had been unchecked. One thing that I did not do was play with God. When I was out there, I was all the way out, I did not go to church and play church.

Although I was finding it difficult to do myself, I knew that it was possible to live a life that was pleasing to God and keep your flesh under subjection because Paul said so in 1 Corinthians 9:27. He said you must do it through "discipline".

While in Germany I sat under enough good teaching to know that there was a spirit attached to me that had not been dealt with appropriately, one I had not been delivered from. Something still had me and put not only me in harm's way, but my children also. You see, the wife found out about us and while I was on my way to Florida to pick up my two youngest children from summer break, she went to my house. My baby brother Courtney, my son Corey and daughter Shona were there. God only knows what they said to her because they did not tell me. I can only imagine the three of them standing in the doorway looking like the Cosby Kids minus Fat Albert, talking stuff. They did not play when it came to mama.

I remember the phone calls as we were on the road. The first one from the children telling us that she came by and they think she had a gun. The second one was from him with her screaming and yelling in the background. She had him at some hotel hemmed up supposedly threatening his life. I started to tell him to tell her to go ahead and shoot him and put both of us out of our misery but I didn't. The third call came from her. I told her where I was and what I was doing and that when I returned we could talk. I thanked God that I was not home–not because I was scared but because she probably would have had to use that gun if she had one considering the fact that she disrespected my children. Though her move was gangsta, I understood that sometimes the rules in the game of love change and you have to pay the cost to be the boss-lady. The group Brownstone had a song that said "In the game of love you either win or lose but you have to face the truth when you play the game of love". Though I was no longer a "thug-ett", I was out there far enough not be punked. Since we both were being forced to face the truth, I began to prepare myself mentally for the showdown.

Needless to say the trip to Florida seemed to take forever. My mind was all over the place. Thank God my sister was with me. We made it to Florida safely and spent the night and we were back on the road early the next morning. I knew I had to end the foolishness quickly so I arranged to meet with the wife the following day. She and I stood in my front yard as I took responsibility for my part in it all; I admitted that when I found out he was married I should have left him alone. I asked her how she found out about me and where I lived. She told me that one of their mutual friends told her about me. He had come to my house several times so I knew exactly who he/she was. I could not figure out what was up with all the homeboys snitching. The guys in Little Rock obviously didn't know that snitches get stitches like the guys in Louisville.

The pain that I saw in her face was the same pain that I am sure others saw in my face as I endured a cheating husband. The same pain that I caused Brandon years before and "the wife" even farther back than that. I shared information with her that she knew that only he could have told me, intimate things. It was those things that hurt her the most. The saying holds true that "hurt people, hurt people". After the shock of my words wore off she spoke these words to me "he must have really cared for you to share those things about me to you". In that moment, I not only saw her pain, I felt her pain. As if to put me back in check, she began to share with me that I was not the only one but that there were others. She told me that he was into "young" girls and that there were several young girls that he was messing around with in the apartment complex where they lived. One of them in particular confessed to her face that they had been together on multiple occasions. This young lady had gone as far as to describe his sexual prowess blow by blow—Ouch! Children can be so cruel.

I asked her why she stayed with him despite all she knew. She looked me straight in the eyes and said "because I love him". They had been dating since high school, parted ways and had found each other years later and had married. She had three children from previous relationships but was unable to have a child by him. If the truth be told I couldn't judge her and neither can you. We've all done some stupid things for the sake of so called "love".

The door had been opened and the familiar spirits were having their way. I had gotten caught up in the way that the world did things again, the way I had done things in the past. I had drifted so far from being the person that I was in Germany that I did not recognize myself as that person anymore. Death had knocked on my door yet again but God did not allow me to be there to catch the bullet.

Unbeknownst to Will, God spared both of our lives that year. There were some disturbing suspicions his wife shared with me concerning he and her oldest daughter that caused me to question *her* mental stability for real. There were some things I found out partially that year and fully years later that would have caused him to be in his grave and me in prison smoking Newports and serving a life sentence. Ladies, be careful what you let in your house around your daughters and sons.

1 Timothy 4:1

"now the Spirit expressly says that in latter times some will depart from the faith, giving heed to deceiving spirits and doctrines of demons..."

*H*e's *Intentional*

*I*t's amazing how when things go bad, we know how to run, and run fast back to the place that we know there is or should be safety…the church. I sought and found the little storefront church by Al's Fish market that I visited with Brother T, —Led by the Spirit of God Church. The first thing that I did when I got there was officially repent for all of the wrong things that I had done.

After visiting a few Sunday's and allowing the Word to cut me to pieces, my family and I joined. It was a Sunday morning in 1998 and my new Shepherds were Pastor Al and Monique Montgomery. Led by the Spirit was more like the church in Germany than any other that I had visited in the city. It was a small church and the Word was good. Pastor Al's enthusiasm and energy reminded me a lot of my former pastor, Pastor Fitzgerald. Pastor Fitzgerald was a white pastor with a black congregation but if you did not see him and only heard him, you would think he was black. He would begin his preaching on the floor but when the Holy Ghost kicked in he would sometimes end up standing in a chair or pew. Pastor Al was the same way.

I knew I needed to get busy in order keep my mind occupied and my flesh in check so I volunteered to help out in any way that I could. My first official job there was placing Pastor Al's glass of water and two peppermint on a small table by the pulpit- that was it. It wasn't a large role, actually it was a very small role, but it was the role God had given me. He had me back in training, only this time I wasn't fighting demons, I was learning how to serve the man and woman of God.

When I first went to Led I didn't realize that residue of the streets was still on me. Although I cleaned up pretty good, the stench of sin was still on me. My pastors recognized where I was but still took me under their wing to groom me for ministry. I'm so thankful that they were not religious but spiritual in nature with a genuine love for God. Religious people look at the outer appearance, spiritual people look at the heart.

While back under the safety of a spiritual umbrella I was quickly finding that my greatest battles were not fought with people, my greatest battles were fought within myself. TD Jakes referred to my condition as "the enemy–in me." No one knew of my past life prior to getting saved, not even my pastors. Though trying to turn my life around, I was still loaded down with a lot of baggage. Some of it belonged to me and some belonged to others. No matter how hard I tried I could not seem to break free from the things that had me bound. In Romans 7:19, Paul said *"For the good that I would I do not: but the evil which I would not, that I do."*

My prayer soon became that not only would God set me free, but in the midst of it, reveal His intentions for my life.

Proverbs 3:7, 8
"Do not be wise in your own eyes; Fear the Lord and depart from evil. It will be health to your flesh, and strength to your bones."

The Cost of the Call

I threw in the towel after the Will fiasco and was concentrating on church, family, school and work—in that order. Tashona, Katecia and Jeremiah were doing well and I was enjoying being a nana to my granddaughter Tionna. Corey was doing his own thing and flying below the radar; he was surely his mother's son. In the beginning it was hard for me to pray and sleep well at night when Corey started staying away from home. Although God's Word constantly reassured me that He knew exactly where Corey was; it was God reminding me that He is "omnipresent", (everywhere at the same time), that taught me how to pray and rely on Him to watch over my children. Nothing can be hidden from an "omniscient" (all knowing), God.

Just like the rest of us who moved out and thought our mom didn't know what she was talking about, he too found out that *mother knows best.*

I was going to church on Wednesday nights and Sundays and it appeared that I was back on my spiritual "A" game. I began weekly counseling with my pastor and started praying and asking God to deliver me from the soul ties that I had with Lee, James and Will. I began to read my bible, study the Word and write sermons just like old times. Although I seemed to be back in the groove, I still did not truly have inner peace.

Over the course of time, Pastor Al saw that God had His hand on me and confirmed that there was indeed a calling on my life to share God's Word. Through my counseling sessions with him

I began to realize that it wasn't really even about me. I was placed on earth with a purpose and for a purpose. However, the self-respect and love that I denied myself caused me to allow men to become my vice. When I thought on it, I could not understand why God would want to use someone like me. It was not until I started dissecting my bible that I began to understand. David, Paul, Moses and Peter were four of the greats and though they had issues, God used them. They brought glory to God's name through the things that they suffered and overcame and that is what he wanted from me.

Even though I was back in church and was truly in love with God, I was messed up, dressed up. Romans 10:9 says "That if thou shalt confess with thy mouth the Lord Jesus and shalt believe in thine heart that God hath raised him from the dead thou shalt be saved." I had confessed and believed in Him back in 1992, yet there was still something missing. It was years later that I caught the revelation of "progressive sanctification". Progressive sanctification means that even though you are saved, you will go through a process. You are not *sinless*, but you should be *sinning less*. That revelation alone can cause a person to rest in God more and beat themselves up less.

I didn't understand fully what was going on, but my soul was in the middle of a tug of war between my flesh and my Spirit and for the most part, the flesh had been winning. The lifestyle I lived in the past was not conducive to receiving the best from God but because He knew the plans He had for me, His grace gave me what I did not deserve and his mercy kept me from getting what I did deserve.

I once heard that pure, life changing ministry is birthed out of humility. If humility produces anointing, I was next in line to receive a double portion. The bible says that iron sharpens iron. I thank God for sending me a prayer partner.

1 Peter 4:17
"for the time has come for judgment to begin at the house of God; and if it begins with us first, what will be the end of those who do not obey the gospel of God."

Sister-Friend

One day while I was picking Jeremiah and Katecia up from their afterschool care, I saw this little lady that I would run into on occasion around the school. She was always pleasant and even though she was not a teacher, I noticed that she was always smiling and interacting with the children and the children seemed to love her. Katecia told me that she worked in the cafeteria and that her name was Mrs. Rosalyn. Her daughter, Gynesis was in her class and was her best friend.

Due to my tight budget, I was looking to get the children out of the afterschool program and have someone trustworthy to watch them for a couple hours until I got off work. I didn't know it at the time, but Mrs. Rosalyn lived only a block from the school and only a few blocks from my house. I had agonized over asking my neighbor whose children attended the same school as mine to watch them but we never really talked or interacted with each other. My other neighbors were a couple that did not care much for us because of our dogs "Bout it and Shaq." "Bout it" belonged to Corey and was a pit bull and "Shaq" was mine, a Rottweiler and Doberman mix. Shaq was cute as a puppy but as he got older he had a face that only a mother could love. I think those neighbors were the ones that poisoned Shaq but I couldn't prove it. 'Bout it ran away after getting tired of Corey's Shenanigans. Corey had him tied to the house with a 2-foot chain but he somehow got loose in the middle of the night and ran for dear life. I personally think that the poor dog wiped away his own tracks so he would not accidentally end up back there.

Before Shaq died Corey bobbed his tail with a rubber band–who does that? There are too many "Corey" stories to recount from those days so I will just say he was tha bizzness!

One day while I was at the school I saw Rosalyn and out of the blue I was led to stop her and introduce myself. I told her my situation, how much I could afford to pay and asked if she would consider watching Jeremiah and Katecia for me. She was very polite and told me she would ask her husband that night and would let me know the following day. The next day when I saw her, she excitedly told me that she would be able to do it. The rest is history…

Rosalyn and I started out just chatting when I would pick up the children in the evenings but eventually we began to confide in each other more and more and became really good friends. I began to love her children, Broderick and Gynesis as they were my own and she loved all of mine as well. Even after I no longer needed her to watch them for me, I would walk pass her house on the way to the school to pick them up and I would hear a pecking on a window and it would be her beckoning me to come over and talk to her. She had such a great sense of humor and would have me laughing so hard I would sometimes lose track of the time. Just like we shared many laughs, there were many tears shed between the two of us as well. Those were times that bonded us like sisters.

It was through my friendship with Rosalyn that God began to show me how important my witness was. Through our conversations, I found out that we came from totally different backgrounds. She came from a large family, whereas I was the oldest of 5. She grew up in the church and I did not. She was married and I had been divorced twice. She had two children and I had 4. Although in the beginning it appeared that we did not have anything in common, after discussing our love for God, we found out that we had the most important thing of all in common, our Father.

Rosalyn's Baptist background and my charismatic one gave us plenty to talk about. I remember the first time she went with me to a Sunday night deliverance service at Trumpet and Zion Church. I loved going there on Sunday nights when our church did not have service because it truly made me feel like I was back home at Patton Christian Fellowship in Germany. Though I felt at home, this type of church was different for Rosalyn. She was a little frightened at first, but before the night was over, she was unmistakably enlightened to the realness of God. A deposit was made and she was never the same.

I never invited Rosalyn to Led, she invited herself. I knew that she was already attending another church and after her experience at Trumpet and Zion, I wasn't sure if she would be comfortable at Led. She came one Sunday and then another and then finally she joined. We began to pray together and fast together. The same tongues that had once startled Rosalyn, could be heard coming from *her* mouth. She began to operate in the Spirit and witness awesome manifestations/deliverances take place in the lives of herself and her family. She also began to dream and interpret dreams. Despite the spiritual levels we were on, at times trouble would still find us. In spite of what some may say or think, *"being saved"* does not mean that you are exempt from trouble. If the truth be told, there will be seasons that we all will go through where there will be more trouble than we ever had in the world. The good news is Jesus Christ. Although it may seem like He is nowhere to be found, His Word declares that He sticks closer than a brother and will never leave or forsake us.

Unbeknownst to Rosalyn, while I was praying her through a situation, I was seriously struggling in my faith walk at that time. The pressures of being a single mother, bills and life were taking a toll on me. I was not truly happy and I was not reciprocating what I was giving out to so many others. Well you know that the enemy only needs a crack. My emotional state had opened me up for a valley experience like none I had experienced since I had given my life to Christ. Another trap had been set for me and I walked right into it—literally. Not even my prayer partner could discern or intercept the curve ball that the devil had coming my way.

Ecclesiastes 4:9, 10

"Two are better than one; because they have a good reward for their labour. For if they fall, the one will lift up his fellow: but woe to him that is alone when he falleth; for he hath not another to help him up."

The Curve Ball

When I first met him he was sent over to the Heart Hospital through a temp agency to wash dishes. According to my job description, I was to assist the food service and environmental service departments as needed. I mostly coordinated the weekly caterings for meetings that the president or finance officer held. This meant that I was often in the kitchen with the cooks and servers. I did not think much of *M.C. when I first saw him, he was not my type at all. He would work there a few days and would not be back for a few days so in passing we would speak and that would be it. When he was there I would often see him in the hallway or cafeteria with one of the ladies from housekeeping so I figured they were trying to develop some type of relationship.

Our conversations started out very casual and increased to deeper conversations due to his transition from dishwasher to an actual cook for the hospital. Since I worked directly with the food service department we saw each other more. He eventually asked me for my number and if he could see me outside of work. He appeared to be a gentleman so I agreed and we began going out to dinner and for rides around the city. Our relationship started out pretty slow but quickly progressed. I noticed that as our relationship progressed, I started straying away from church again. Although I tried it—I had pastors that cared about me and my family and when they did not see me at church over a period of time they would call or show up at my house to find out why. Just like always, I couldn't hide anything from Pastor and ended up spilling my guts. Pastor Al did not go! Because I had begun confiding in him about my previous relationships and a little bit of my past, he did his best to convince me that my new relationship was merely another distraction to get me off track again. Although Pastor gave me great counsel, I did not want him to be right, I really thought that M.C. would be a keeper.

M.C. confided in me early on that as a child his mother took him and his brother to church, however he was no longer a church goer. That *should have* been my cue to run like Forest Gump but instead I sat there and listened while little cupids swirled above my head like in the cartoons. He told me he had once lived a pretty interesting life at one time but had turned over a new leaf and was on a different path. He was both street smart and business smart. He loved drinking Heineken Beer and cheap champagne, smoking Capri cigarettes and eating romantic dinners at nice restaurants. It was via M.C. that I started back smoking cigarettes after not smoking for 7 years. It started by taking puffs off that little skinny Capri cigarette of his and before long, I started having him to leave me a few. The day he forgot to leave me a few was the day I ended up buying myself a pack. Just like that, I was hooked again.

I could tell that once upon a time money had not been an object to him because of his appetite for the finer things in life. Although he was no longer balling, he got the best inexpensive things he could find. He had dreams and he had goals and we would talk for hours about ways to make money and how we would start our own businesses. Though I had only introduced him to my sister, brother and Aunt Annette who jokingly nicknamed him "Mugsy", a cartoon character, my children liked him and he was the first one that I felt could actually fit in with my family.

M.C. and my relationship remained for the most part casual and did not actually go to the next level until he invited me and a co-worker friend of ours and his boyfriend on a trip to New Orleans. It was some type of festival weekend but not Mardi Gras and there were people everywhere as we walked around the French Quarter. We went on a swamp tour on Saturday and watched big burly men bait and pull alligators out of the swamp waters, shopped at the mall and hit the clubs that night. It was the perfect weekend and believe it or not it was the weekend that I finally fell in love again. I did not think anyone could take Solathian's place in my heart but M.C. not only took it, he stole parts of it that I had not let any man, including Solathian, have.

A month or so later I went to his hometown and met his family. He and his mother were very close but his and his father's relationship seemed strained. He was close with his brother but did not seem to be close to any other family members which was strange to me since I had a very close knit family. The conversations we shared while there gave me a clearer understanding as to why he acted the way he did.

Over the following months our love grew stronger. He would give me cards filled with cash and flowers just because. He doted over me by taking me out for romantic dinners, buying me gifts and making sure I had everything I needed or desired. He respected me and my children and basically became everything that I dreamed that a husband should be. He was a true gentleman, a great lover and I was head over hills in love with him. There was not a doubt in my mind, I knew that he was the one that I would spend the rest of my life with.

Before long, he was spending nights at my house and I was

hanging out at the apartment that he shared with a friend. It was when we no longer liked not being able to wake up and see each other first thing in the morning that we began to feel that we were ready to take things to the next level. We decided that it only made sense for him to move in and help me since I was buying my home. Being at home would also allow me to spend more time with my children. Although my children were not strangers to seeing a man spend the night at my home, no one had ever moved in and shacked out there. The thought of letting him move in bothered me the most because I knew that if he moved in I would totally stop going to church again. It was bad enough that I had backslid and let God down, I was NOT trying to go face Pastor Al.

While we were still indecisive about living together, M.C. and I began to discuss marriage. Sometimes we were feeling it and other times our insecurities from past failures interrupted our talks. Although he had never married, a lady that he was once in love with ended up hurting him and it left scars. He did not want a repeat and neither did I. Slowly but surely more of his things ended up at my house, A shirt here, a pair of pants there, yet he had not (in the words of Beyonce) "put a ring on it".

Just when I thought I was getting close to covering all bases in regards to my family life I received the call that no mother wants to get concerning her teenage daughter. I got a call from the school nurse saying that my oldest daughter was pregnant. I did not even know school nurses were authorized to give pregnancy tests without parental consent. I had just pulled up in front of the bank to make a deposit for the hospital when the call came in. As the nurse was trying to explain I could hear Shona crying in the background. Ignoring the nurse, I asked to speak to her. As my crying child got on the phone I tried to calm her by letting her know that she would be okay, the baby would be okay, we would be okay. I personally knew how scary it was and how bad you feel to be pregnant at such a young age. I did not want to make matters worse by making her feel abandoned by her mother.

In light of the situation, I let her know that I loved her and that her child would be a blessing. Although there were a lot of questions to be answered and doctor appointments to be made, I knew that just as God had been there for me, He would be there for her. Unfortunately, there is a time that we must all pay the piper for our indiscretions and my daughter was not exempt.

In the midst of me trying to be "every woman", the enemy had gotten a foothold and was attacking my children. Subsequently, I saw the cracks that I left open for it to happen. Away from the house a lot, not really paying attention to what was going on at home, in my own world, "doing me". Ladies, this is a *cautionary* truth so please beware.

In the natural realm, I thought I was in the big league- winning! Despite the curve ball that had come my way, I still felt I had hit a home run with M.C. I didn't realize that in the spirit realm it was already Striiiiiiiikkkkke 1!!!!!

John 15:5
"I am the vine, ye are the branches; He that abideth in me, and I in him, the same bringeth forth much fruit. For without me ye can do nothing."

Another One Bites the Dust

 $\mathcal{M}$ ajor changes took place at the hospital and Marriott lost their contract. We were left without any one to manage the food service departments so M.C. and I stepped in and began to reset things up from scratch. I taught him everything that I learned from Marriott and within a couple of weeks, we had most of the vendors and service contractors back in place. Since there was a job opening for a manager to oversee those departments, they sent someone over to train M.C. for the position.

When M.C.'s finances appeared to be lining up the way that he wanted them, out of the blue he asked me to marry him. Though we had only known each other a little less than a year, we decided that our love was strong enough to make it work. On January 8th, 1999 we had a justice of the peace come to our home and marry us. The children were not present and the wife of the justice of the peace was our only witness.

M.C. made us reservations at the Excelsior Hotel and we stayed in one of the top of the line suites which came complete with complimentary champagne and room service. Because the room was so expensive, when the room service attendants came to bring us our food they asked if we were rappers. They noted that the only people of our persuasion that stayed in rooms on that floor were rappers. They did not know that M.C. was balling, but on a budget.

The night was awesome and the months ahead were awesome. The month of April was especially awesome because my second granddaughter, Jahkori Renee Ticey was born on April 4th, 1999. It was an Easter Sunday which made her the blessing God told me she would be. It was also her great uncle Courtney's birthday which makes it special in so many other ways. I had never witnessed an Easter being that early in the month so I believe that it fell there just for my Kori. She looked so much like me when I was a child that I nicknamed her "mini-me". She immediately stole another piece of my heart.

It took a minute but before long my happiness quickly began turning into sadness as M.C. began to have dreams that would cause him to wake up in a sweat. Dreams that he was falling and his mother and I were trying to save him. The children and I started back going to church and I had been praying that he would join us and rededicate his life. One Sunday I convinced him to go with us and almost immediately during altar call Pastor honed in on him and called him up. A prophecy came forth by Pastor that was right on the money. I could tell by M.C's facial expression that he knew that he had been exposed and that it was God speaking. Needless to say, he never wanted to go back. Although he did not say it at that time, Pastor Al saw something dark in him that I did not see. Later during one of our counseling sessions he told me; yet I still refused to *see what I was seeing.*

When I initially got married, I justified my marriage to myself and to Pastor with the scripture "it is better to marry than to burn" which was totally out of context. Needless to say the scripture rings true "how can two walk together unless they be agreed" and "do not be unequally yoked with unbelievers". We were unequally yoked and not walking together which meant double trouble.

The next months were very hard and things began to change. He complained that I was changing and I argued that he was changing. No longer were the date nights—I was always too tired. No longer were the back rubs, sweet conversations and cuddling—I was always sleeping. I could not understand what was going on with me. He became to me like kryptonite is to Superman. Before long he began to start hanging out with a couple of the guys from work and after only six months of marriage, I came home one afternoon to him crying as he was taking his clothes to his car. I went into the house and saw the rest of his clothes on the bed instead of in the closet. I asked him what he was doing and he stated "I can't live here anymore". I quickly thought back to just a couple weekends before when I did not go out with him to a club that one of our mutual friends invited us to. He got upset and decided to go alone. That night he did not come home. I did not know if he was hurt, in jail or laid up with another woman. When he finally came home, he came with flowers, a card with a hundred dollars in it and an apology. He swore that he stayed over his old roommates' house because he was mad at me but my gut did not buy that story.

What he did not know and what I did not want to admit was that God was dealing with me also. It's as if as soon as I said "I do", the noose around my neck got tighter. It was one of those things you try to ignore, but as women, we know what we know even when we don't want to know. So much was going on in my life. Jeremiah was continually acting up in school, Corey was going through some things, Katecia was dreaming dreams and they were coming to pass which was kind of scary, Tashona had a baby and I was about to go through *another* divorce.

My pastor never approved of the marriage nor gave me his blessing concerning it because he knew that it was not God's will.

He felt that if it had been, I would have shared it with him before, not after the marriage. He knew that he was not only my pastor, but my brother in Christ and that there had to be a reason I kept it a secret from everyone.

Maybe it was the look on M.C.'s face after our I do's or the fact that we could not consummate our marriage on our wedding night or the fact that I shut God out and let M.C. into my life. It was obvious that by walking in the flesh there was no way that the marriage could be God's perfect will for my life. There was nothing that would cause God to get the glory out of it. One thing that is so awesome about God—He will take that mess up and make it work together for your good.

The saying is true, "Sometimes God will let you hit rock bottom to let you know that He is the ROCK at the bottom." For some of us, that is what it will take.

Deuteronomy 31:17

"... Then My anger shall be aroused against them in that day, and I will forsake them, and I will hide my face from them, and they shall be devoured. And many evils and troubles shall befall them, so that they will say in that day, have not these evils come upon us because our God is not among us?"

Torn Between Two Lovers

Chapter IV

Karma is a Witch

*C*rushed to the tenth power, confused to the maximum degree, hurt to the extreme, lost and without hope are just a few of the words that I can use to describe this period in my life. What I can tell you without a doubt in my mind is that Karma is a female and she is a witch.

My dreams of having the husband, white picket fence, a career and children had been dashed again. While trying to manipulate my *process*, I failed to consider that it's like taking a knife to a gun fight when you go up against a sovereign God. Silly me, I still had not learned that my interference would prove to be the source of many delays in my life. How dare the clay try to direct the hands of the Potter?

That afternoon as I lay on my bed in a stupor, I began to hear the still small voice of God. God was saying, "Twana, your life is not your own… You will not be able to have it your way.. You are chosen… You are called… I handpicked you…Surrender to me fully". All I could do was lay there and cry.

Over the following weeks I often caught glances of M.C. in the hallway and saw those that had spoken doom over our marriage conversing in corners. Our co-workers had predicted the fate of our marriage from the very beginning and the predictions were not favorable. Single ladies did not respect the fact that our divorce was not finalized and neither did he. I caught him flirting as he walked around like a proud peacock in his new position as the "HNIC" over the three departments. It was a position that I helped groom him for—all the way down to the fresh haircut.

Shortly after Marriott's services were terminated and in order to avoid a conflict of interest, I had been moved into the hospital's accounting department. It was while working in that dept. processing checks that I ran across M.C.'s hospital issued phone bill. I noticed that there were a lot of phone calls to a non-hospital number so I wrote the number down. We had been apart for about 3 months and I could not believe that he was already talking to someone else. Neither of us had filed for divorce and had spoken of possible reconciliation on more than one occasion. It was hard to dismiss the number of calls made to that same number so I dialed it. Just as my gut had warned me, a female answered the phone. After a brief conversation explaining who I was, I got off the phone with the young lady who had been gracious enough to confirm my suspicions that they held conversations; yet she insisted that they were merely friends. Feeling angry and betrayed, I called M.C.'s office and asked if he could meet me in my old office and he agreed.

We talked for a minutes and then I asked him to dial a number for me. He dialed the number, not realizing at the time what the number was until he had dialed all 7 digits. As soon as the female answered and he recognized her voice, he hung up. He was light-skinned and his face turned the darkest shade of red as he looked me straight in the face. He was speechless for a moment and then said "whatever man" and turned for the door. I asked who she was. He began to get angry and headed out the office. When I grabbed his jacket, he looked at me and said "nobody." As I continued through tears to ask more questions, he said "man, I gotta go" and left the room.

Just like that, I knew that it was really over. My friends in the world would say, "You know what goes around comes around". The Word of God says "Be not deceived; God is not mocked: for whatsoever a man soweth, that shall he also reap." (Galatians 6:7) Read your bible—it's the truth, the whole truth and nothing but the truth.

Colossians 3:25

"But he that doeth wrong shall receive for the wrong which he hath done: and there is no respect of persons."

Big Bank take Little Bank

Over the following days I stopped eating and became smaller than I had been before the birth of Jeremiah. I hated going to work because I knew that I would see him there happy and smiling. I began to wonder if he had only used me to help get him a better position there and never really had any intentions to stay with me. After all, he had not told his mother about our marriage in the beginning. Hmmm, that sounds familiar. I spent my lunch time and breaks sitting outside feeding my nerves with Capri cigarettes and consequently fell into a deep depression.

The feeling of hopelessness began to overtake me to the point that I recall being at work one day, thumbing through the yellow pages, looking up psychiatrists. I felt like I was about to lose my mind just like I had when I took the pills back in Fort Benning Georgia so many years before. I did not want spiritual counsel, I wanted someone to feel sorry for me and say 'let's lock her up in here for a while until she can get herself together'. I finally found an office that was near the hospital and arranged for an appointment. A couple of days later I went and sat face to face with the man that I thought would make all my pain go away.

I will never forget it was a Wednesday evening and as I began to pour my heart out, the doctor sat there and listened intently. After I snotted and boo-hooed for a while, he handed me a tissue and asked me this question, "Do you feel like doing harm to yourself or to others?" I knew that all I had to say in order to get committed was "yes" but when I opened my mouth to say it, I said "no". The doctor looked at me stunned and I looked at him stunned. He proceeded by asking me if I went to church and I told him yes. He told me that I needed to go to church that night and ask God to give me peace. Really? Even though I knew he was right, I didn't want to go to church, I wanted someone to take care of me. As he continued to reassure me that everything would be alright, I was sitting there thinking, out of all of the psychiatrists and psychologists in the City of Little Rock, how did I end up with one that knew God? Reluctantly, I took his advice and visited a church that night. The Word that came forth was just for me. The person that spoke had no idea that his powerful words were being used to give me enough strength to face another day.

A few days later, M.C. and I ran into each other again in my old office. He began to share with me information that the HR Manager shared with him. It was a private conversation between she and I, yet she shared the gist of our conversation with him. In that confidential conversation I shared with her the possibility of me leaving the hospital due to my failing marriage. As an HR Manager, she was out of line for sharing a conversation I shared with her in confidence with him or anyone else. She had been someone that had assisted him in his transition to manager and someone that possibly liked him a little more than she wanted me to know so I understood her motive. M.C. was a manager so he had the juice–I was replaceable.

I could not believe that that someone in her position had done this, so I went to her office to find out why. As I sat there in tears, I told her what M.C. told me and asked her why she shared our conversation with him. Her face turned as red as M.C.'s turned when I made him dial the phone number just days before. She was speechless for a few moments. I'm sure she was wondering why he told me, not realizing that in cover-ups, it's every man for himself. Being the *professional* that she was, she quickly regained her composure and apologized profusely. She also realized that her job security was on the line so she began to think quickly and came up with a brilliant plan. She offered to have a check cut for my full pay, back pay, plus my vacation and sick pay if I would go ahead and quit that day—you know, to relieve the stress. Of course she used a little more tact than that with her words, but the results were the same. I signed the papers and they cut me a check, a big check. The ancient proverb holds true, "the fish rots from the head".

My last day at Arkansas Heart Hospital was August 13, 1999. I was too distraught to drive, so M.C. dropped me off at home and wished me the best. If an umpire had been present, he would have yelled—Striiiiiiikkkkkkeee 3!!!!

James 4:4

"Adulterers and adulteresses! Do you not know that friendship with the world is enmity with God? Whoever therefore wants to be a friend of the world makes himself an enemy of God."

He Had to Reach Waaay Down

*T*he children were still in school when I made it home so I went into the house, went into my bedroom and fell onto my bed. I was so mentally and physically exhausted; I must have cried for hours. I felt like I had been in *A Rumble in the Jungle* boxing match with Muhammad Ali. First, he had me on the ropes… then he used the rope-a-dope… the Ali shuffle… a swift uppercut… and right before the bell rang ending the 1st round… he knocked me out!

I was lying there asking God why He allowed it to happen. He had been a good husband. We could have worked out our differences. The Lord spoke to my spirit and said "he was a good husband, but he was not your husband." Wow! Needless to say, that weekend and the following week was filled with many tears and many prayers. There were times I felt as if I was completely losing it. But every time I looked at my children I knew that I had to hold on a little while longer.

The following weekend I went down home to celebrate my grandfather Arthur's 88th birthday with my family. Time with my family proved to be therapeutic as I was reminded during that weekend that I still had much to be thankful for. I had never introduced them to my husband, not once had I taken him to meet my family. It dawned on me that weekend that I'd been on borrowed time from the beginning. In my desire to remain transparent, I must confess that deep within my soul I knew all along that I wasn't going to be able to keep him.

I recall the days and weeks that followed were long and the money was short. I was without a job and was having a hard time trying to find one. My planner from that period shows that I sent in application after application and mailed resumes on a regular basis. I had a couple of interviews but nothing ever transpired. M.C. would come by on occasion and drop off some money and because we were still married, sometimes we did *grown folk* stuff. He was having his cake and eating it too as I desperately prayed that we would work things out. It did not take long to figure out that I was the only one feeling that way as he shared with me one day over the phone that he was filing for divorce and that he had been talking to lawyers prior to me leaving the hospital. When I thought back I recalled being in his office one day and seeing 1/9/99 written on a page in the opened phone book that was lying on his desk. That was NOT the day we got married but it was too close to it not to realize that something was up.

Although it was not what I wanted to hear, I made up my mind that I would not contest, my only request would be to go back to my former last name, "Nuniss." The entry I wrote in my planner September 7, 1999 read, *"Broke off ties w/M.C. trusting totally in the Lord to supply for my every need".*

I shared the news with my pastor and he prayed for me. Although he was not surprised, he didn't say "I told you so." Instead he prayed that God would give me the strength to endure my wilderness. He also reiterated that there was a call on my life and that there was nothing I could do to abort it. Pastor Al and Pastor Monique were very instrumental in my comeback. They prayed and made sure my family and I were okay. They did not always tell me things I wanted to hear, but instead they pushed me to do better and to stay kingdom minded. Pastor Al was very straight forward and didn't hold back on what needed to be said. He showed tough love and I thank God that he did.

I slowly began to start talking to God with some sense. I mean, I was never disrespectful but I did ask a lot of why questions. While I was wallowing in self-pity and pain, God began to deal with me. The entry from my planner dated September 16, 1999 read, "...*God turn the hurt I feel into something positive. Please don't allow me to go there again....*" I put myself on a 5-step program because five is the number of grace. I decided that my first 2 steps would be to start praying more and start smoking less.

It was actually my brother Ed that brought it to my attention. Every day I would call and ask him to drop me off a pack of cigarettes on his way home from work. One day when he came, he had two packs. He told me he bought two so I would have one for the next day. A spirit of conviction came over me that day so I prayed, and asked God to help me quit just like He had in Germany. Unfortunately, it didn't happen instantly like it had back then.

A little at a time, God began to show me that the source of my hurt did not just come from the break up. There were still things inside of me that had not been dealt with. One morning I woke up and I felt my spirit leaving my body—I mean literally. The only way that I can describe the feeling is as pure as a ball of cotton looks, is as pure as the feeling that I felt in that moment. It was a clean that does not compare to what we know clean to feel like and it only lasted a few seconds. I could only imagine feeling that way completely and forever. After that experience I was fully persuaded that our loved ones in heaven do NOT want to come back down here. With a feeling like that, who would?

The next day, I was sitting in the tub taking a bath and crying when I began reflecting on different childhood things, in particular when my mom and dad would fight. Even though my pre-teen and teenage years had been filled with some turmoil, as I got older I assumed that the past was just that, the past. I did not understand that unless you get delivered from a thing, you are never free of it and that the things that you are most afraid to reveal/or face about yourself are the things that have you bound. As I sat there thinking on these things, I began to feel the presence of God.

During what seemed like an hour but was only a few minutes, I cried for the little hurt girl that was inside of me. When the cry was over, I knew in my heart and felt in my soul that the little girl was finally free. As I wiped my tears away, I could hear with my spiritual ears God saying that it was okay. Then, all of a sudden, I stopped hearing and God stopped speaking.

Consequently, the next days and weeks I stayed buried in my bible. I was reading, fasting and seeking God's face. It's amazing that the very things that we know to do we don't do until we are put in a position where that is all that we have left. In spite of all that God does for us, we are simply too selfish when it comes to giving Him our time. Sundays should not be the only day that we pray or seek His face. I love the song from back in the day that says *"I need thee, o Lord, I need thee, every hour, I need thee....."*

I was at my lowest place and He had to reach waaaaaay down to get me. Thanks be unto God for Jeremiah 1:12 which says *"Then said the Lord unto me, thou hast well seen: For I will hasten my Word to perform it."* God had begun a work in me and was obligated to finish it—by any means necessary.

Mark 4:7

"... and some fell among thorns, and the thorns grew up and choked it, and it yielded no fruit..."

The Silence of the Lamb

It seemed as if it came without warning, but if the truth be told, there were plenty of warnings. The fact of the matter was I ignored them. As God remained silent, I remained lost. Once you have tasted how good He is and when He is seemingly absent from your life, you miss Him. Most importantly you realize how much you really need Him. In God's silence, He spoke to me through His mercy. I woke up each day able to get out of my bed, I had food to eat, I had my mind, although I can't say it was my "right mind" and my children were healthy and well.

In His silence, His grace was sufficient towards me and during the silence, I still felt Him near me. I knew that He still loved me and that there was nothing that I could do nor was anything that I had done that would stop Him from loving me. The more I thought on those things, the louder the silence became.

Weeks passed by and I longed to hear God's voice again. I longed to know the plans that He had for me. I longed for Him to share secrets and mysteries with me. I finally understood why Jesus felt forsaken yet not afraid on the cross. The sins he carried for us separated Him from God and He missed hearing His Father's voice.

I have since discovered that when our Father is silent, He is perfecting our faith, loving, correcting and/or healing us. Even in His silence He is still being the God of a second chance and a third chance and a fourth chance and a fifth chance… it doesn't matter how many we need, He is the God of *another chance*.

Psalm 86:15

"But thou, O Lord, art a God full of compassion, and gracious, long suffering, and plenteous in mercy and truth."

The 4th Inning

There have been times in baseball's history where the evidence of victory did not appear until the 4th inning. This became even more apparent to me when without my permission, God took over my life and began to heal me and restore it.

Suddenly, I realized that though I had been a casualty in the war of love, not one, not two, but three times, God still had my back. The facts of the matter were that the plans God had for my life would not allow me to be in a marriage that was not ordained by Him. I could not truly experience the fullness of Him while operating in my flesh and I never would be able to. I didn't know it but God's plans for me were far greater than anything that I could have ever imagined.

In the natural, my situation still looked ugly and I still could not see the light at the end of the tunnel. I had however received something that I had not had in a long time. I had received some P-E-A-C-E!! When God grants you a moment of peace during a storm, you better appreciate it. It's called "Amazing Grace".

Before long I was tapped back in to my "power" source and began to see what I had not seen before. While I was crying and telling God how good of a man M.C. was and asking Him why I wasn't able to have him, I neglected the fact that God knew the man that I married better than I did. As I began to seek Him tirelessly (Jacob), He began to speak to me in dreams first. He showed me the true heart of the man-M.C. There were dreams when interpreted showed that I had been sleeping with the enemy.

There was one dream in particular that showed M.C. completely out of character. He was wearing shorts while standing in a line to get food in the hospital cafeteria. I say out of character because M.C. never wore shorts in public. God showed me in that dream that he was about to be exposed. The most shocking dream of them all was the dream where I saw this apartment building and as I looked inside of the upstairs apartment, there was a little girl crawling around on a couch. The child was between six and seven months old. The Spirit told me that the child was the daughter of someone that M.C. was dating. I called him that next day and told him about my dream. As I shared the details of my dream, he was dead silent. Then he admitted to me that he was indeed dating someone that had a six-month old daughter and she lived in a second floor apartment. I was flabbergasted. Not that he admitted it, but how precise the dream had been. God did not stop there but continued to show me the intentions of M.C.'s heart. He also showed me that he was never intended to be my husband, he had merely been an assignment.

The dreams launched me further in to my process. It did not happen overnight, but it came one night through prayer. I asked God to release me from the soul tie that I had with M.C. I asked Him to forgive me for my sins, for putting not only M.C. but the three previous guys I had been with ahead of my relationship with Him. I also asked Him to heighten my discernment so that I would be able to see the true intentions of a person's heart. I knew that God had forgiven me and had granted my petition as soon as I ended the prayer. I also knew that there was a judgment attached to my sin and that there would be a price to pay for laying down my cross.

I was thankful that my fate did not lie in the hands of man but in the hands of a merciful God. Despite how it looked to the natural eye, in the spirit realm I was WINNING!

1 Samuel 16:7

"But the Lord said unto Samuel, Look not on his countenance, or on the height of his stature; because I have refused him; for the Lord seeth not as man seeth; for man looketh on the outward appearance, but the Lord looketh on the heart."

The Pursuit of Holiness

$\mathcal{S}$olathian and I had been communicating more over the years and had gotten over most of our differences. We were talking one day and I told him about my impending divorce when he shared with me that he was about to get married. Because I was so distraught about my own situation, neither jealousy nor envy came to surface and I was genuinely happy for him. I gave him my best wishes and prayed that he would have better success than I had.

I was getting back on track at church, Sunday mornings, Wednesday nights and any other time I could get in the door I was there. I don't care what anybody says, getting whipped with a wet switch will put something on your mind—if not yours, it did mine.

According to my journal, it was October 15th, when I called Pastor Monique and told her that God had been dealing with me about sharing my testimony. On the 3rd Sunday night of each month Pastor allowed people to minister and share what God had put on their hearts, it was called, "Sunday Night Rain". I knew that it had to be God because I did not like public speaking. I was led to ask for the 3rd Sunday night in November. When I realized that November was the month and the 3rd Sunday was the Sunday that I had gotten saved in Heidelberg Germany, I knew God was up to something. Pastor Monique told me that she would talk to Pastor and get back with me the following day. The next day she called and it was confirmed that November

21st, 1999 would officially be my first "sermon". It was exactly 7 years from the date (November 22, 1992) that my spiritual journey had begun. Look at God! Though my spiritual life was improving, I still needed God to work things out concerning the natural things, like bills.

I kept getting shut off notices for my electricity, yet they never came to turn it off. The first thing to go however was my car. The same car that a year earlier had been taken by Corey and my baby brother Courtney on a late night adventure. The adventure resulted in them blowing out a tire and parking it in an apartment complex parking lot a few blocks away. At that time, I had not sent in my payment but I was not behind so I could not understand why they would come and get it. I called the dealership and they said they did not take it. I was about to call the police when the culprits volunteered to go and look around the neighborhood and question people in the area. Coincidentally, they were able to find it. They were too big to beat when they finally confessed to that one.

Losing the car made finding a job even more difficult. My friend Rosalyn would sneak and let me keep and use her car while she was at work. My sister would take me places when she was not working and I even used my brother's truck "ghost rider" *once*, I couldn't handle ghost rider. ☺ With all that was in me I kept on pushing.

I received a call from Pastor Monique one day telling me that Pastor wanted me to attend a ministers meeting on October 26th. She also let me know that one of them would pick me up. The following weekend my aunt Annette came in town and spent the night. She blessed us with food and gave me $10. That Sunday I was led to sow the $10 Annette gave me into the building fund. It was all the money I had, but I was obedient. That afternoon after church, my Aunt Linda and Uncle Carl stopped by and gave me a check for $300.00. Because I was walking by faith again, God was "causing men to give unto my bosom". It was one thing for God to touch a person's heart, its' another for that person to be obedient. Shortly after that, a lady from the church gave me 2 large bags of clothes. I had lost so much weight that nothing I had fit anymore. A few days later I received a letter from the insurance company saying that they owed me money from 1998 in the amount of $340.00 but it would take 3-4 weeks to get it. I prayed it would come sooner.

With the money I received, I was finally able to pay on some of my mounting bills, buy food and meet some of the needs of my children. God met me at my crossroads and began blessing me in the midst of my situation. The more I pursued Him, The more He poured out His blessings.

Over the years I had not had many interactions with my biological father, but God began to deal with me concerning that. After my car was repossessed he was in town and came by to check on us. A couple days later he came back and told me he had a little car that I could use if I needed it. I really did not want it but thanked him for his offer. It was that night that God revealed the resentment that I secretly held in my heart towards him. It was not malicious, but it was resentment nonetheless. God told me that I had to free him in order to free myself so I cried about it and prayed about it and vowed to try. I still didn't take the car though.

Sometimes while pursuing holiness you can be in a storm where God has you so protected that you can't tell you're in one. God doesn't stop the storm and He doesn't rebuke it; He just gives your wings enough strength to fly above it. Thank you Jesus!

Isaiah 25:4

"For thou hast been a strength to the poor, a strength to the needy in his distress, a refuge from the storm, a shadow from the heat, when the blast of the terrible ones is as a storm against the wall."

The Best of Times, the Worst of Times

*I*t was on November 18th, 1999 that I received my divorce papers in the mail; it was also my Aunt Annette's birthday. Just two days prior to receiving them, I ministered to M.C. over the phone. During the conversation God gave him a warning about some things M.C. had going on coming to the light. In order to make a believer out of an unbeliever, God spoke specific things that only He and M.C. could possibly know about. The divorce papers were stamped the very next day which further assured me that the devil was still on his job. M.C. used irreconcilable differences as the reason for our divorce and even had a guy that I had only met once be a witness for him. I did not contest it and just as we had agreed upon, we each left the marriage with what we came in with. He did not try to take my house, though it was community property, he simply wanted his freedom and I gave it to him. I also was given the one thing that I requested—my former last name "Nuniss".

God is so amazing. He takes our broken pieces and one by one He puts us back together again. The fight that was in me was still too weak and the reminder of the pain I went through was still too strong to take my chances outside of God so I stood still, I had no desire to get back into the ring.

I continued to look for a job and yet I could not find one. I was 3 months behind on my mortgage payments and they were sending me pre-foreclosure letters. I considered bankruptcy but didn't know how it worked, so I went and talked to an attorney. He told me that I could not put my house in bankruptcy because I was not working at the time. I did not know what to do, so I did nothing. I had 3 children and a granddaughter that depended on me. While they depended on me, I depended on God.

November 21st came and I ministered my first message— *The Purpose and The Promise*. I had been fasting and praying over that message for weeks. I shared my testimony as well as how I found that there is purpose in our trials and tribulations. I expounded on the fact that there is nothing that can negate the fact that God's promises are Yay and Amen and that He keeps the promises that He made to *Himself* concerning us. I was also able to testify that God had once again delivered me from cigarette smoking. Hallejuah! That night during offering time Pastor Al took up an offering for me and my family and placed his check from the church in the basket as well—seeds sown.

The next day, I received another shut off for my lights. I paid on them with the money I received but it still was not enough to catch that bill up entirely and pay the other bills. It was the 4th extension Entergy had given me since August without me asking for one. But God!

Thanksgiving finally came and we went down home. While there, God allowed me to speak into the lives of my grandmother, mother, sister and aunts that day, it was a specific word for each of them. He allowed me to do it that particular day because my time with M.C.'s last name was coming to a close. Coincidentally my grandmother's mother had the same last name as M.C. That last name held significance in our family because my grandmother's mother died when she was a little girl. I learned that day that something as simple as a last name can break a generational curse.

Later that night I went to a prayer meeting with my best friend Deborah at my Cousin Pearlie's home. Pearlie is a very meek and quiet woman but when she opens her mouth to speak, she reveals the prophetic mantle that is on her life. That night she prophesied to me, "You will be running an organization working with kids. I see you running it out of a building". Per my journal, she went on to say "God said to lay out all of your bills and pray over them and that you will not be walking much longer. He is going to bless you in your own business—going to houses. God is going to pay off your debts. "I cried, I rejoiced, I praised and I received it!

The next days were filled with ministry down home. While being led by the Spirit, I went from house to house praying and speaking into the lives of those that God led me to. When I returned to Little Rock I laid out my bills and prayed over them just like the prophetess had told me.

Isaiah 55:11

"So shall my word be that goeth forth out of my mouth; it shall not return unto me void but is shall accomplish that which I please and it shall prosper in the thing whereto I sent it."

TORN BETWEEN TWO LOVERS

CHAPTER V

He Made A Way

God began to deal with me more and more in dreams and most of them have already come to pass. M.C. and I spoke cordially on occasion but whenever he propositioned me for sex, I had to tell him like BB King, "The thrill is gone". Although legally he was still my husband, the late night hook up sessions were ova! God was dealing with me and challenging me to go higher. The closer I got to God, the more I was able to resist the temptations that came my way. The more I denied my flesh, the more my flesh went under subjection. The following Sunday a prophecy came forth that I was about to go under attack again... Two days later, the electricity got shut off. *Dat Blast It!!!!*

I remember the day so vividly. Rosalyn was walking with me to my house. As we turned the corner to my house, we saw the Entergy truck in front of my house. Immediately, Rosalyn looked at me and began to cry. I reassured her that all was well and that we were going to be okay. I knew that God was still God lights on or lights off. The next day the phone was cut off. My faith had grown by leaps and bounds and nothing was shaking me. It was a Friday night when my brother came over and told me he was going down home and that we could stay over to his house for the weekend. While I was over there the Holy Spirit reminded me that the shed that was in my back yard was on a different electrical circuit than the house. When I returned home on Sunday, I ran a large electrical cord from the shed to the house and hooked up my television, lamp and electric heater and made it do what it do.

Almost one week to the day of the prophecy, God instructed me to pray over my bills again. I also wrote down the type of car I wanted for good measure. I was instructed to literally sweep out my house and to continue to stand in faith. Any doubt, anxiousness or unbelief would only hinder what God was doing behind the scenes.

One day I put in a Juanita Bynum tape, prayed and then for some reason I wrote... "My blessing has landed". After staring at what I wrote for a minute, I looked at the clock and it was time to go and get Katecia and Jeremiah from school. There was laundry that needed to be washed so I gathered the clothes, put them in a backpack and started out the door. As I turned to lock the door behind me, I noticed that there was a receipt taped on the door. It was an Entergy receipt showing that the entire bill had been paid—all $800.00. The time on the receipt was around the same time I was writing down my bills. Even to this day no one that I know has been able to take credit for paying that bill—God did it! To top it off—the following day the insurance check came and I was able to get my phone service restored. Can you say supernatural increase? Nothing but obedience to God can cause miracles to manifest in our lives. I shouted and cried and gave God all the glory. I will share that testimony for the rest of my life. The miracles did not stop there, food boxes showed up on my door step and money was being placed in my hands. God's mercy was evident and I knew that I was standing under an open portal of blessings. Because I was properly aligned, the blessings flowed freely.

The scripture the Lord gave me during that time was psalm 23. The part that says "...though I walk through the valley of the

shadow of death, I shall fear no evil for though art with me…."
ministered to me. Although it had been a trying year, it was still
a good year and I was greatly anticipating a fresh start as we were
about to step into the year 2000.

Matthew 6:33

*"But seek ye first the kingdom of God and His righteousness;
and all these things shall be added unto you"*

Y2K

We entered the year 2000 with the world being afraid of computer crashes and the Coming of Christ. People were storing up food and water, running to church, digging underground shelters and taking their money out of the banks. I wasn't afraid because I knew that God would supply for all my needs. Besides, if it was really the Coming of Christ, I thought I was ready to walk onto the streets of gold. Neither happened (which was good for all of us) and I continued to pray for God's grace and mercy as I continued to walk out my wilderness experience alone.

March of 2000 proved to be a trying month for my family. After what seemed like 100 years, I heard from my mentor, Karan. We had lost contact in the midst of one of their transitions after leaving Germany. Imagine my surprise when one day my phone rang and it was her on the other end of the line. She and her family were stationed in Fort Knox Kentucky which is located about 45 minutes from my old stomping ground, Louisville Ky.

My mother agreed to come to Little Rock and keep the children for me so that I could travel to Kentucky and get rejuvenated, in the Lord, with my mentor. The trip would also be an opportunity for me to see my uncles—John and Charles and my Aunt Vie. I was also looking forward to seeing my Harris family whom I would stay with during the summers as a child, especially my cousin Tanya.

My tax refund arrived right on time and I flew out shortly thereafter. It had been 6 years since I last saw Karan (she and Will were the ones that took me to the airport when I left Germany). Over that weekend we sat for hours catching up and talking about the Lord. We prayed, we shopped and we went to see her daughter Chris play basketball at the college she was attending. I got to see my Uncle John and my cousins and I was regretting having to leave the next day which was a Sunday.

I was preparing for church and packing my suitcase at the same time when I received a phone call from my Uncle John. He told me that my cousin Michael had been shot and was in critical condition. I was in shock because nothing like that had ever happened in our family. When they told me who did it, I was in even more shock. Not only was the person a friend of the family, he had once been in the family and was the father of two of my first cousins. I told Karan and we immediately began praying. We decided to stick with the initial plans that we made which was to go back to Louisville and meet my Uncle Charles (whom I had not seen) at his church. Afterwards, he would be the person to take me to the airport.

When we walked into the church it was packed but somehow we managed to get ushered to the front of the church. The Spirit was moving and the Word was good. The Word was so good and the Spirit was so high that it was not long before Karan was caught up in the Spirit and was in the position that I saw her in so many times before when we were members of Patton Christian Fellowship in Germany—face down on the floor praying and weeping.

After the service was over and we managed to get ourselves back together, I introduced my uncle to Karan and Will and we all headed to my cousin Gerl's house so that I could say my goodbyes. The airport was about 20 minutes away and we were running late. Although I knew I was risking missing my flight, the Spirit led me to have Karan to pray with me and my family for Mike's recovery. After we finished praying, my uncle whisked me off to the airport.

God is so awesome! Although I was late getting to the airport, the flight was delayed and everyone was just beginning to check in. When I arrived in Little Rock, I did not have anyone to pick me up because everyone was at the hospital so I rented a car and went to UAMS to meet up with my family. My Aunt Gwen was doing as well as could be expected under the circumstances but I could see the deep concern on her face. The diagnosis had not been good but she was a believer and she was believing God for a miracle. I had a ceramic piece that my mentor had given me while in Fort Knox. It was a shawl draped over a cross. It had anointing oil on it and I gave it to my aunt to put in Michael's room. Every day the hospital was full of our family and friends waiting to hear some good news. Unfortunately, a few weeks later Michael succumbed to his injuries and went to be with the Lord at the tender age of 25. It was a hard blow to our family but we stuck together and made it through one of the most difficult times of all of our lives. My grandmother had 9 kids and there was a slew of grandchildren and great-grandchildren but Michael was the closest family member to me that had passed away (that I knew) other than my Great Grandpa Will back in the 80's.

Man did not provide justice for Michael's death but we know that the Word of God declares in Deuteronomy 32:35 "To me *belongeth* vengeance, and recompence; their foot shall slide in *due* time: for the day of their calamity is at hand, and the things that shall come upon them make haste." RIL Michael Aaron Joyner.

John 11:35
"Jesus Wept."

Favor Ain't Fair

Although Solathian was married, we communicated on a regular basis in regards to the children. Most of our by-gones were still by-gones and we were slowly becoming friends again. He was still in the military but was also selling real estate and was doing quite well. During one of our conversations he mentioned that he thought I would be good in real estate because I had a way with people. He basically confirmed what the woman of God prophesied months earlier when she said "...I see you going to houses". I believed it to be a good field but still was not sure if it was a good field for me. I trusted that the woman of God had heard from God so I kept the words she'd spoken to me in my heart. God was telling me Greater! Better! Think higher! So after a lot of careful thought and prayer, becoming a Realtor made more sense. It would provide me with the flexibility that I needed since I was getting phone calls every week from Jeremiah's teacher wanting me to come and put him in check.

As I recalled the prophecy and the confirmation, I decided to do some research into real estate as a profession. I told Solathian that I was looking into it and was intrigued even more when he began to tell me how much he enjoyed it and the kind of money he was making. He also made me a promise that he would pay for everything if I agreed to give it a try. After a couple of days of praying about it, I finally conquered my fear and decided to go for it. Since I did not have transportation, I had Solathian to purchase me a real estate course that I could take at home.

The course was through ERA Collins Real Estate and came with VHS tapes and a manual. I began the course one day and got foreclosure paperwork a few days later.

I was saddened by the thought that I was about to lose my home considering all that it took to get it but there was nothing that I knew to do other than pray for a miracle. Instead of allowing the bad news to get the best of me, I decided to use that energy to learn as much as I could learn so that I could pass the real estate exam the first try.

Between studying, I prayed and between praying I studied. I was really enjoying the course and was inspired even more when God revealed to me that selling real estate would be a form of ministry for me. I vowed that I would never put a sale above the quality of service that I provided my clients and that I would always give it all that I had. God began to show me that not only would I become a Realtor, but one day I would have my own company. I began studying with the mindset of an Owner/ Broker (Boss) from the moment that God revealed that to me. It was as if it had gone straight in my spirit and took life.

Although going through his own thing, Solathian encouraged me every step of the way. Unfortunately, just as my marriage had ended in six months, his marriage was heading in the same direction. I prayed for him and for his family to be restored and truly meant it. We had gone in different directions and I was okay with it finally. Although I remembered the prophecy I received in Germany and the one he received in North Carolina, I lost all hope in it ever transpiring years before.

I must admit, there were times when Solathian and I were on the phone for hours laughing and talking about something crazy

Jeremiah did or what he was going to do with them during the summer that I would reflect back on those days in Georgia when we first met. The times we shared before we got married were the most special to me because they were the simple times. We did whatever it took to be together and did not care what anyone thought about it. Just as the Prophets prophesied, we both had experienced marriage again, just not to each other.

The time finally came and I took the state exam to get my license and passed it with flying colors on my first try. I was elated to say the least although I did not have a clue how I would be able to work anywhere without transportation. I had the book knowledge and the people skills but I knew I would need to gain some field experience in order to prosper in it.

Needless to say, as I was rejoicing from getting my license, I was also in the process of packing to move. The foreclosure process was about to conclude after 3 long months and though I hated to lose my home, I was glad that it was over so that I could move on with my life. I had become so numb to bad news and change that when one thing didn't work out, I merely waited until God did the next thing. In this case, He told me that he would provide me with another place to live and I believed him; after all He is *Jehovah Jireh*. (The God who provides)

Mark 4:8

"...And other fell on good ground, and did yield fruit that sprang up and increased; and brought forth, some thirty, some sixty, and some an hundred-fold"

Rams in the Bush

Like always, God always has a ram in the bush. One of those rams happened to be the Realtor that had previously sold me my house. She had a rental that was available and offered to show it to me. Although there was a park in the neighborhood and it was convenient to everything, the house itself was not the greatest and the rent was actually more than my house payment had been. There were two reasons that I decided to take it. One I had not been able to find anything else in my price range and two, I didn't want to be homeless again. **#wisdom**

Due to my circumstances, I knew that I had to choose a real estate company to work for that was close by and a Principal Broker that would work with me as I transitioned. Lo and behold, my sister Sharonica came by one day after work and told me about a real estate company that was less than 5 minutes from our home named PG* Properties. She gave me the number that she saw on their sign and vowed that she would be my first client. The next day I called and found out that the company was ran by two ladies and not just any two ladies–two Christian ladies and both were brokers. I spoke with the Associate Broker and we set up an appointment for me to interview with them later that week. **#Timing**

Immediately upon walking in the building I felt a sense of peace. One of the ladies, that I will call *Ann, met me at the door. She was the Associate Broker and also took care of all of the marketing for the company. She quickly took me to the office of the Principal Broker who she referred to as not only the Broker, but also her sister, *Liz. Liz told me that it was a Christian based company and that they loved the Lord just like I did. They told me they only had one other agent–a gentleman that worked with them on a part time basis but had plans to expand their business. Although I would be required to be there for floor duty, I was relieved to know that my hours would be very flexible. We hit it off so well that I ended up signing on with them that day. I told them my sister was going to be my first client so as soon as I got settled into the office, we began getting her preapproved for a home loan. **#Rams**

The ladies began to sow into my life almost immediately. They waived fees, bought me gift cards, clothes, anything and everything that I needed in order to get off to a good start. They trained me extensively and walked me through the buying and selling process step by step. They were God sends and I still appreciate everything that God allowed them to do for me. **#favor**

I was still without a car which made it difficult to be able to show any homes so my Aunt Gwen volunteered to give me a black, 80's something Cougar that I nicknamed black cat. It had been parked in her backyard for years and needed a fuel tank and a facelift but it was a car. I did my due diligence and found that the only place that had the gas tank that fit the car was at a junkyard in a little country town up in the Ozarks. I don't believe that there are too many dark-skinned people, if any up that way, so I was a little nervous about going. My sister Sharonica agreed to let me use her car, Bonnie, and I asked my baby brother Courtney to drive me. Talk about sending up prayers before a trip, I did that. I prayed for God to cause the eyes of anyone that was prejudice to see us in the same skin tone as theirs and to watch over and protect us. **#blinded eyes**

It was a long ride on a hot sunny day without air conditioning To top matters off, there was road construction for over half of the trip. Finally we made it there and without having heat strokes. We were looking for the junkyard when Courtney accidentally made a wrong turn on a dead end street. As soon as we turned on the street we saw a group of good ole boys standing around shooting the breeze. Courtney said something to the effect of "aw hell" which was exactly what I was thinking. He couldn't do anything but proceed in order to be able to turn around so he decided to test the waters by asking one of the guys for directions—it could have gone south at this point but the Lord was with us. The guy that approached the car was nice enough and got us on track to the junkyard. As I peeped at the side view mirror, it looked as if they were smiling awful big as we pulled off, like they were up to something. I silently prayed as we headed down the street that we did not end up at a KKK meeting. We quickly found the junkyard, got the tank and got out of dodge. **#protector**

A few days later I found someone to put the tank on and before long I was rolling. It was not at all how other Realtors were rolling around town but I had to work with what I had. Within a month I sold my first home to my sister in the same neighborhood that I lived in. Not only was it my first sale but it was also my first listing. The home was a For Sale by Owner listing and I convinced the seller to give me a try at selling it. He agreed, my sister loved it and I sold it. I call that a 'double up'. **#humble**

Between August and December I sold and listed several homes and the commissions began to roll in. Although commissions were coming in, I was still behind on everything. Since I was selling lower dollar homes, not receiving full commission and not closing consistently from month to month, I ended up having to move again. Fortunately for me, my brokers had bought a new home and agreed to let me rent the one they were moving out of. They even gave me an option to purchase it. **#provider**

As we entered the new millennium (2001), it dawned on me one day that it had been almost two years since I had been in a relationship. The children, church and real estate had me consumed and I was loving it. Led by the Spirit went through some transitions in pursuit of a permanent home but it did not stop the Word from flowing through Pastor each Sunday; he was still checking us with the Word. At this time I was still active in the church and was believing that God would do great things for me through ministry and real estate. My daily prayer was "God bless my efforts—may everything I touch prosper—give me favor with yourself and with man." **#kingdom business**

Although I loved my job, had great respect for the sisters and was very appreciative of all they did for me, God revealed some things to me that I was not aware of at the onset of my employment with them. It takes a love for God and a convinced spirit to be able to stand still during a test. I came to realize that God will sometimes allow you to be in a situation so that he can reveal things to you in such a way that it will cause you to check yourself. I was able to better understand things that I had not formerly understood and though not my cup of tea, God reminded me that we are all capable of doing some things that we say we would never do. Thank God that mercy is shown to he who shows mercy. **#thankful**

Philippians 4:19

"And my God shall supply all your need according to his riches in glory by Christ Jesus"

Upgrade

*A*round March of that year I got a call from Mr. Nuniss asking me if I had gotten a new car. He knew that I had been believing God for that fully loaded Mazda 626 that my sister and I looked at months prior. When I told him no, he said "good". As I was pondering on why he said "good", he proceeded to tell me that God had put it on his heart to give me his car, which was a fully loaded, 2 ½ year old pearl white Acura 2.5 TL. As I began telling him that I could not afford that kind of car and how it would cause further stress on my funds, he knocked me off my feet by telling me that he was going to not only make the car payments but also the insurance payments until it was paid off! Nobody but God can touch a man's heart to do something like that!

Solathian was still talking when I had a flashback to a Sunday a few months prior. I remembered the children and I were about to leave church and black cat would not start. Pastor and one of the other guys had to help me get it started. When it finally started smoke shot high into the sky and all across the parking lot where people were standing and talking. Seeing that I was embarrassed, Pastor reassured me then that God was going to bless me with another car if I would stay the course and believe. I agreed with him and the car Solathian was about to give me was the manifestation of our agreement. There is indeed power in agreement.

When I realized I was still on the phone, Solathian was sharing with me how weeks prior to him calling me, God had spoken to his spirit about giving me the car but he ignored it. He said that he could not understand why God would tell him to do something like that. On the day of the call as he was pulling out of his driveway, he struck his brick mailbox and it left a long scratch on the front passenger side door. He said he pulled back in the yard and called me because he knew that it was a warning from God. We made plans to meet in Florida at his mom's house in order for me to pick up the car. Later that month, I rented a car one way and the children and I left bright and early one Saturday morning. I could not believe that he was actually giving me his car but when I got there, he really did.

The first time I sat in it tears came to my eyes. God was still showing me favor even after all that I had done. Although I strayed away time after time, He still showed compassion towards me. It didn't matter that Solathian and I had been at odds with one another, God still used him to be the one to bless me with a car—I thought that was pretty amazing.

When the time came for us to leave and as we were heading up the street from his mom's house two birds swooped in front of the car and somehow became entangled with one another. All of a sudden they hit the windshield hard on the passenger side and blood splattered over it. I stopped in a panic and immediately began to rebuke the devil. I told him that he was a liar and that the car was MY car and we were going to make it back to Arkansas safely in it! As I continued to plead the blood and rebuke the devil, God spoke to my spirit and said that it was not the devil. The blood from the birds represented a covenant that he was making with me that no hurt or harm would ever come to me in that car and it never did. Over the following weeks and months I shared my testimony with anyone and everyone that would listen. Won't He do it?

As long as I was close to God, God was blessing me both spiritually and physically. It was only when I stepped out too far from under His covering that I would experience difficulty.

Psalm 34:19

"O fear the Lord, ye His saints for there is no want to them that fear Him."

The Quiet before the Storm

Everything appeared to be on track in my life. I was learning the real estate process and was doing fairly well selling homes. If I had multiple homes closing it was all good, but when there was only one on the table and I was faced with a 30 day wait to close, I would fall behind. I was a tither and I wasn't frivolous with money, I just had more expenses than money most times.

I was working in the youth department and everywhere else I was needed in the church. During times when I was not being consistent in my duties, it would not be long before I would get a phone call from Pastor Al or Pastor Monique checking to see what was going on with me. To make me more accountable, Pastor began training me in the *duties* of an "armor bearer". Though I was not an official "armor-bearer", I learned about the huge responsibility and spiritual significance of the assignment. My role consisted of me praying for Pastor Al and Pastor Monique and ensuring that everything that they needed was where it needed to be before and after service. It may not sound like a big deal but when God puts you that close to the man and woman of God, He has ministry planned for your life.

I'm almost positive I was in my front yard mowing the grass on September 11, 2001 when I got a phone call from someone asking me if I was watching the news. The person on the other end of the line told me that the twin towers had been hit in New York and that another plane crashed outside of D.C. that was believed to be headed to the White House. I ran to the TV and watched in dismay as people were literally running for their lives. Some jumped from the burning buildings while others stood in shock watching the aftermath of the plane's destruction. My heartfelt thoughts and prayers immediately went out to the people of New York.

The news reporters were reporting that it was a terrorist attack and that there were possibly other targets. I began to not only pray for the people of New York, but the world. Never had I witnessed anything remotely like that and I pray to God that I never witness anything like it again. Due to the massive loss of life, unbelievers began to pray and give their lives to Christ. It's sad that it takes tragedy to get our attention. Though God did not send the attacks, He was able to get some glory from the many that dedicated their lives to Him during that time. My prayers continue to go out to those that were affected by/or lost loved ones on 9/11.

Things were going fine at PG Properties when God began to deal with me about leaving. Almost immediately I started preparing to get my broker's license. While I was trying to move forward with my career, the ladies got a buyer for their home that we were living in. I wasn't mad because I knew all along that their intentions were to sell. Though I loved the home, I was not in the position to purchase it at that time. I moved into another house not far away with Katecia and Jeremiah; this was house number 6 since moving to Little Rock.

Before I sold my first property, I knew that one day I would run my own company. I just didn't know how or when. Going solo was not anything that I wanted to do without knowing for sure that it was time. I began to pray and ask God which company He had chosen for me to work at during the interim.

Within a couple of weeks He led me to call Truman Ball and Associates. I knew that it was the Lord that put that company in my Spirit because as soon as I called Truman and told him I was looking for a new home he said "alright girl, come on over and talk to me." I set up an appointment and went a few days later.

When I went through the door, I immediately noticed that there were not any people in the office that looked like me. A few uncomfortable minutes later I met with Truman. As soon as we began to talk, all my apprehensions left. He was a wonderful man and I knew that I would learn a lot under his leadership. Truman told me that he did his research and saw that I had not been in the game very long but had been having relatively good success. After talking about the short and long term goals I had in relation to real estate, he invited me to be a part of *The Ball Team*. I told him that I needed to speak with my brokers but loved the idea of joining his team. From the very start I made it clear to Truman know that one day I would be starting my own company. He told me that he would give me his blessing.

Truman was a millionaire and God was placing me in his path to learn everything that I could. Not only would I learn how to run a company, I would see firsthand the work ethic that it would take to be successful. The bible says that "your gift will make room for you and bring you before great men" (Prov. 18:16). Prophecy after prophecy had been spoken over me that I was destined to be a millionaire. I would visit a conference or a church and if a prophet was in the house and he or she called me out, somewhere in the prophecy "millionaire" and "ideas" would come up. I had no idea how it would come about, but I claimed it each time it was spoken in Jesus name.

The following day I talked to the ladies at PG Properties and gave them my two-week notice. They were believers so they understood; when God tells you to move, you need to move. They were good to me and I prayed for God to bless them per the kindness that they had shown towards me. I learned a lot while working under them and learned a lot about myself.

I began working at Truman Ball and Associates around April 2002. I was told by an agent at another company that I was the first black to ever work there. I don't know if that was true or not because I never asked. I was just happy to be in the place that God wanted me to be.

It had been 2 years since my divorce had become final from M.C. and I vowed that number 3 would be it–no more husbands. There were people that seemed to think that Solathian and I would get back together but I didn't see that happening. I was convinced at this point that the prophecies we received were simply off. After all, even the best of them miss it sometimes, or so I thought.

Ecclesiastes 3:1
"To everything there is a season, and a time to every purpose under the heaven..."

Pastor's Prophecy

I usually had monthly counseling sessions with Pastor Al. During one of our sessions we discussed the possibility of me heading the Single's Ministry. He felt that my life experiences more than qualified me to encourage and motivate other singles. I liked the idea of being a part of a singles ministry, but I did not like the idea of heading it. Pastor recognized my hesitance in accepting the position and changed the subject by asking questions about Solathian. Pastor had met him earlier that year while he was down visiting the children. Being that Pastor was my spiritual father, he did a spiritual check up on him. He later told me that he believed that Solathian was still my husband and that we would get back together one day. Solathian and I were cool and all but I was still a tad bit salty about how our relationship crashed and burned so I wasn't really trying to hear that. I shared with Pastor that for a long time I secretly held on to the hope that we would reconcile and be together again as a family but my hopes were dashed again and again as he and I both went from relationship to relationship. Pastor was not at all convinced and told me so. I simply replied "O.K. Pastor."

It was around July 2002, I don't recall if it was a Sunday service or a Wednesday night service when Pastor prophesied to me. He told me these exact words "before the end of this year, you will know who your husband is without a shadow of a doubt". I got excited! I was like really God? You are giving me a husband? I've sat still long enough for *You* to send me my Boaz? I wondered if God was going to send him to Led or if I was going to be out somewhere and he come up to me and say "God said you're my wife?" or maybe I would be visiting another church and he would see me there. I couldn't figure out any other way he would find me other than at a church.

All during the service I was excited. I left the church excited and even the next day got excited when I thought about it. As days passed by, the prophecy was placed on a shelf and forgotten.

I don't claim any type of attention disorder but I am hyper. Most days my mind would be all over the place. One business or non-profit idea after another. Trying to do everything and not seeing enough positive results. Because I wasn't consistent in branding my ministry or business, I was not seeing the success in real estate or my nonprofits that I desired to see. Needless to say, I began to get discouraged; whenever I got discouraged, I started slacking.

It was December 31st, 2002 when I received the phone call. I was lying on the couch asleep when the phone rang. I recall looking at the clock and it was 11:50pm. I answered the phone and it was Solathian and he was crying profusely. It scared me because I thought that someone in his family had died or something. He kept trying to say something but I could not make out the words and then finally he calmed himself enough to say, "I called to tell you I'm sorry and to ask you if you would marry me again". I said "What?" I kept asking what was wrong. I thought—this must be a joke, what is he talking about? After continuing to ask him what was wrong, I gently told him that he was just upset and that we probably shouldn't try marriage again. Almost instantly, he regained his composure. He tried to explain what he was saying but he didn't really know what he was trying to say himself. A few minutes later we got off the phone and I laid there wondering—what just happened? I didn't know it at the time, but Solathian had been under spiritual arrest.

It was only a few days later that the Holy Spirit reminded me of pastor's prophecy. Pastor said "Before the end of the year you will know who your husband is without a shadow of a doubt." The opportunity had presented itself just like I had been prophesied to in Germany, Solathian in North Carolina and most recently by my pastor. Because I lost faith in the prophecy, I missed my opportunity to "enter in" just like the children of Israel.

Instead of living as husband and wife in a marriage that was prophesied to be "better than ever before" Solathian and I continued to live single and apart. I couldn't even blame the devil for that one.

Habakkuk 2:3

"For the vision is yet for an appointed time but at the end it shall speak and not lie; Though it tarry, wait on it; because it will surely come, it will not tarry."

Torn Between Two Lovers

Chapter VI

Ministry birthed through Humility

$\mathcal{T}$hough I still loved real estate, I was not finding the success at Truman Ball and Associates that I had hoped for. I found myself becoming intimidated by the success of others and would often retreat home after only spending a few hours in the office. I had shut off notices for everything and my household was suffering tremendously. I remember slipping in such a deep depression that one day I literally got in my closet, closed the door and cried for hours. I was broke, exhausted and at the end of my rope. About an hour later Solathian called and told me he was putting money in my account. We were still connected in the Spirit and God used him to bless me financially on so many occasions during that time that I cannot count them all. He would send me hundreds of dollars at a time and paid bills for months at a time. On one occasion, he put a thousand dollars in my bank account because he said God told him to. He bought me a laptop, a camera, paid real estate fees, and just as my cousin Pearlie prophesied about God paying off my debts, one day he called me to let me know he was going to pay off some of my debts. He did all of this in addition to paying child support. Although he wasn't my husband, he was better to me than "10 husbands" at times.

Though I could not do the things he did for me financially, I was there for him spiritually. I encouraged him as he continued to pursue his education. I prayed for him as he went through his divorce. I was a sounding board for his ideas and a liaison between him and our children. Gradually I saw God healing our relationship and we became friends again.

It was 2003 and the Joyner Family had been truly blessed to have suffered only a minimum amount of loss from our family tree over the years However, we found out early in 2003 that my grandfather Arthur, (whom I affectionately called daddy) had been diagnosed with prostate cancer. We all watched him as he went from a vibrant and happy soul to one that was dealing with the weariness that cancer causes. The girls and mama (grandma) cared for him and I would go down on weekends and sleep on the floor beside his bed. I was not there when he passed away, but he was surrounded by his daughters who say he pointed toward heaven when he saw the angel that came for him. When they looked back at him, he was gone. He was 93 years old. I said a few words at his funeral and recited the scripture that I often caught him reading from his small bible, it was John 14:2. I truly believe it was his favorite. Jesus was speaking to the disciples in John 14:2 when he said "In my Father's house there are many mansions: If it were not so, I would have told you. I go to prepare a place for you..." How befitting was that?

A piece of my heart went with daddy that day. He was the Patriarch, our rock and one of the most creative men I have ever known. He didn't like for his children to fight or be at odds with one another but taught us to love each other. His legacy lives on through us and I know that he is smiling down from heaven on us as we stand together "Joyner strong" just the way that he taught us. Rest in love daddy.

I learned from the things that I suffered, it made me more adamant about ministry. Although hesitant and afraid at first, I began to teach the singles ministry. I realized that it was meant to be when God gave me an entire year of messages for the class. We met regularly on Wednesday nights and even planned and went to a Woman thou art Loosed Conference in Dallas that changed all of our lives. Bishop TD Jakes ignited such a fire in me that I really did *get loosed* and began to share my testimony through my Wednesday night messages—no holds barred. As I began to share, the more the people began to respond and the more relieved I began to feel. It was then that God prompted me to start keeping a journal and chronicle my life experiences. I was to start with my earliest remembrance.

When I started writing, I used the journal as my way to reveal the things to God that I could not reveal to anyone else. There would be times that I would get on my computer and type for hours at a time and cry. When the cry was over, I felt so much better. Because my new-found freedom felt so good, the next time I wrote, I shared even more of my deepest, darkest secrets with Him (as if he didn't already know.)

I made it a practice to save my work on a cd that I kept tucked safely away. Once I accidentally left the cd in my computer and Solathian was in Arkansas visiting. He got on my computer and the journal was still up so he read a portion of one of my entries. It upset me because there were many things about me that he did not know and that I did not want him to know. Like I said earlier, the things you are afraid to reveal are the things that have you bound. There were things in the journal that no one besides myself and God knew and that's exactly the way I planned on keeping it.

Eventually, I began to be a part of the ministry team and helped with the media ministry as well as with the youth. Every place that I could serve, I served. My heart however was with the single's ministry the most because of the commonality that we shared. My testimonies helped them and theirs helped me. I always felt that a singles ministry should be led by a single person—someone that could tell me to hold on because they were holding on. To *me* it didn't make sense to have someone that was going home to big biceps and triceps laying in their bed every night to be up telling single women, "just hold on baby, your Boaz is coming." Don't get me wrong, I believe that everyone's witness is important. However, I feel that the content of a message is more authentic when it comes from someone living the life that they are preaching about.

I was ordained in ministry in 2004. My mom and my aunts came from down home and listened intently as I shared what God put in my heart that day. Though I was nervous, I believe that my message blessed the people. While at Led, I found out who I was to God and so many things about myself—both good and bad. Pastor Al and Pastor Monique were my family and always would be. Though they nurtured me and my children for 7 years God began telling me that it was time for new beginnings—He just didn't tell me where.

There had been several times during my journey at Led that I found myself missing the mark and sitting myself down. Through counseling sessions with pastor, I would eventually get in line and take my position back with the other ministers. I did not sugar coat my slip-ups. Yes, I slipped off to see the strippers with someone that had on a rabbit coat and thought everyone was laughing at her (you know who you are) and yes, I would often try to abort my calling and meander back into the world.

Though stronger than when I first arrived at Led, there were still times that I fell weak.

I must admit that my last trial before leaving Led temporarily set me back. During that trial, I found out that people's actions and manipulations can leave an already broken person even more broken. What's understood don't need to be said, so I shall leave my mishap exactly where it is, covered by the blood. My pastors and cohorts continued to encourage me in my walk with the Lord during my trial. They saw on me what I could not see–the anointing.

The force I was fighting was spiritual and on any given day, it could get the upper hand on me if I allowed it to. Though I had my share of Bozo's instead of Boaz's, there had not been a person or thing that messed with my mind the way the enemy did. I suffered with suicidal thoughts, feelings of worthlessness and hopelessness. Though my faith was not on fleek at times, I knew that there was something awesome that the devil was trying to keep me from.

During some of my lowest points and darkest days, I would log into my computer, pull up my journal and pour out my heart. As I fought back the tears, I began to see my life as if I was on the outside looking in. For the first time, I could pinpoint the experiences that shaped my life, both positively and negatively. Neither I nor the devil knew the purpose behind that revelation.

Isaiah 42:16

"and I will bring the blind by a way that they know not, I will lead them in the paths that they have not known. I will make darkness light before them and crooked things straight. These things will I do unto them and not forsake them."

Back to the Basics

There were some major changes taking place in my life and I was on the upside of the mountain. I knew that 2005 would be a better year because I was hearing God clearer. I claimed victory over my mind battles and felt that I was on my way to a better life. The first order of business was to go to speak to my pastor about leaving the church. Although, I knew that it was of God, there was a hesitation to present it to my pastors. I decided to take the coward's way out and called Pastor Al on the phone. Pastor was not convinced that I heard correctly and told me that he would pray about it. I hung up the phone and continued to drive. While driving, the Holy Spirit confirmed to me that it was indeed time for me to leave—my assignment was over there.

It was a Wednesday night and God directed me not go inside of the midweek service—I was to wait outside in my car and pray. When the service was over, I went inside. There were people still standing around talking and Pastor was sitting on the steps that led to the pulpit, dripping with sweat. When he saw me, I could tell that he knew what I came to do. I walked over, handed him the keys and gave him a hug. I then went over and gave Pastor Monique a hug and told her thanks and I loved her. She embraced me and told me she loved me too and to take care. I walked out of the church and my Spirit felt at ease. I was wondering what was in store for me next when I was reminded by the Holy Spirit that "8" is the number of "new beginnings"

A couple of Sunday's later the children and I were invited to Longley Baptist Church by Rosalyn. I didn't know what to expect but as the children and I walked in, I felt good about it. Longley was formerly Rosalyn's home church and her parents had been members there as well. When we walked into the Sanctuary I looked up and there was a huge banner that read, "Back to the Basics". The Holy Ghost let me know from the jump that I was about to go through a spiritual boot camp.

Matthew 4:40, 41

"And he said unto them, why are ye so fearful? How is it that ye have no faith? And they feared exceedingly, and said one to another, what manner of man is this, that even the wind and the sea obey him?"

Something old,
Something New

I liked Longley Baptist Church because it had a mixture of young, old and those in between. My children also seemed to enjoy it and the Word was always good. After visiting a few Sundays, we not only joined but signed up to get baptized as a family.

One of the things I especially liked about Longley was the fact that it was a Baptist church and I would not be called on to minister. Generally, women did not minister in traditional Baptist churches and I was almost positive that Longley would not be an exception. I never really liked pulpit preaching, I was always more comfortable sharing my testimony in the streets. I have read stories of people that were once strung out on drugs or were once drug dealers that when God touched their hearts, they turned their lives around and have led thousands of people to Christ. The things those people experienced and were willing to share are the things that caused unbelievers to believe.

It was March of 2005 when I left Truman Ball and Associates and started Nuniss Realty and Investments. Our slogan: "A Company Investing in People". The company's startup costs were financed by Solathian and an investor that I had been working with for years. The 1500 square foot building I acquired was in a great location and was right down the street from Led Church. Initially it was up for sale but God gave me favor with the leasing company and I was able to negotiate a lease with an option to buy. My first year was free and my rent was $300.00 per month with the 2-year option. The building needed a lot of work and money had to be used wisely, so I did a lot of the painting, and decorating myself. I also put down the carpet because a woman has to do what a woman has to do.

As I sat at my desk in my high back chair looking around at all that God had done, I thought back to 2003-2004. I had taken a class downtown that was offered through the Small Business Administration and UALR. It was an entrepreneurial training class that taught us how to put together a business plan for our potential businesses. God had already spoken to me about what he wanted me to do so it was a no brainer that I take the class. During our last class, we were told we would have a ceremony that would be recorded and televised on one of the local T.V. channels. They wanted us to vote on different things such as who would have the largest company, who would be the first millionaire etc. Well at the ceremony when the category came up for which company would make the first million, my peers voted for Nuniss Realty and Investments. There was maybe $10.00 in my purse and no money in the bank as I stood before the crowd smiling and holding my plaque. That day as I looked around my office, I claimed millionaire status.

Around September of 2005 I got the news about Truman. The receptionist from his office called and told me that He was very sick with a very rare, life threatening disease. It broke my heart because he was such an awesome guy. I remembered the huge smile on his face when I told him about my new office. He gave me his blessing and told me that I could call him if I needed him; six months later I was attending his funeral. As I approached his wife at the cemetery, she turned to me and gave me a big hug and said "he was really fond of you." I told her that the feeling was mutual. Truman was a believer so I look forward to seeing him again one day.

As fate would have it, whenever I got involved in *anything* more than I was involved in Kingdom business, all heck would break loose! It was summer and the children were gone to be with their dad and I found myself not only having to move, I became homeless again.

Unfortunately, there had been a couple of clients whose financing fell through and all my savings was depleted. A few nights I slept in my car in the parking lot of Baptist Hospital and other nights at my office. I didn't want anyone to see my car up at the office or draw criminals, so I didn't stay there very often. It was Arkansas hot so I knew I couldn't continue to sleep in my car. I talked to a friend and she agreed to let me stay at her place temporarily. I knew I would have to do something before the children got back home from their summer vacation so I started hustling to get more clients.

One morning I got out of bed and was heading to my friend's kitchen when I saw her on the back-porch smoking on something that had once been near and dear to my heart...Mary Jane. It smelled so good and I was feeling so bad that I walked out on the porch and asked her if I could hit it. She was shocked, but quickly obliged. After we got through smoking I got the bright idea to go to my office to do some cold calling. I was so high that I could barely see. As I drove, I would use the license plate on the car that was in front me as a guide to stay on the road. I could not have been going more than 20 mph down University Avenue when I began to hear demons saying over and over "we got her now...we're going to kill her today". At first I thought I was just tripping, but when I realized that I was *really* hearing voices, I got scared. I turned the radio to the Christian channel to try and block them out. As the gospel music blared, I began to pray and ask God to protect me and not let me die. By the time I pulled into the parking lot of my office, my high was completely blown. A 10-minute drive had taken me 30 minutes. I sat in my car and thanked God for not letting the devil kill me. I felt like I had just been in a thirty-minute episode of the *Twilight Zone*.

Job 1:12
"And the Lord said unto satan, behold all that he hath is in thy power; only upon himself put not forth thine hand. So satan went forth from the presence of the Lord."

Wild Thing

Although initially I was disappointed in myself, I could not deny that I enjoyed the feeling I felt when I was high. The weed I was smoking was much more potent than what I smoked with Lee's sister. It was so strong in fact that I could only take a couple hits. I thought it was laced with something, but I think it was just "loud". My friend's boyfriend was a big smoker and kept her supplied so eventually the two of us began to smoke on a regular basis. Both of us were goofy so we would smoke, laugh and then eat up everything in the house. I stopped going to church completely and started getting my own stash and hiding it at my office.

Eventually I got another house back in my old neighborhood and it was much nicer and a lot more spacious. My daughter Tashona was living in Alabama and was due to have my first grandson that September so I knew that I had to get myself together. I was so excited when she told me that she was finally having a boy. My weed smoking went on for about a month and then it was as if God said, "you know what…"

I had several clients that I was working with and deals on the table prior to starting to smoke. As soon as I started smoking consistently, the deals began to fall through, one after the other. I will never forget the day that I had an encounter with God in my office. I had gotten high, sprayed perfume, brushed my teeth, put visine in my eyes and was about to leave for the day when the phone rang. One of the few clients I had left called me concerning their file. I started not to answer but thought, oh it will be okay and answered anyway. Usually, I was pretty cool when I was under the influence, but this day as I spoke with the client, I stammered over my words. I couldn't remember details of the file and I sounded very unprepared and very unprofessional. Somehow I got myself together and gave them the information they needed and got off the phone. As soon as I hung up I felt the presence of God fill the room. As I stood by my desk I heard God telling me that if I didn't stop, I would lose my business and that He would expose me. Then suddenly I started walking very slowly to the back of the building where I kept my stash. I was screaming and crying all the way. That demonic spirit did not want to be delivered but the Holy Spirit let it be known that it was about to go down. Holding the small bag of weed in front of me and walking like some type of mummy, I headed to the restroom. Reluctantly, I flushed the bag down the toilet. As the Spirit released me, I cried and I cried and I cried.

God delivered me that day in an instant. My high was completely gone and I did not desire to smoke weed nor did I get weed from my friend again after that day. God had mercy on me and I did not lose my client but gained another. The guilt and condemnation I felt was the greater punishment. God did not condemn me, my guilt condemned me.

Shortly after the incident at the office, the mind battles began *again* and I was ready to throw in the towel. I didn't share the experience I had in the office with anyone. Just like most church people, I didn't want to be judged. For weeks I thought back on that experience. It was one of several encounters that I had experienced since being saved that reassured me that God was real and that He had no problem dealing with me on a personal level.

God always gave me a way of escape and that escape came in the form of a trip to Alabama to witness the birth of my grandson. Tashona gave me the privilege of naming him so I named him Micah. Micah means *"One who is like God"*. After his birth, Tashona and her other two children, Phylashia, and my mini-me Jahkori moved back to Little Rock with me. The house was filled with excitement and grandbabies. Their presence during that season revived me and brought meaning and joy to my life again.

D.H. Lawrence
"I never saw a wild thing feel sorry for itself. A small bird will drop frozen dead from a bough without ever having felt sorry for itself."

Living Suspended

$\mathcal{T}$he next couple of years were like a blur. I was working towards my Associates degree and was still sporadically selling real estate. I was trying to get a regular 9-5 job but I couldn't get a job blowing bubbles. Tashona was in her own place and the children were doing well. Solathian was still there for me whenever I needed him and my family members were all doing well. I was attending Longley Church on a more regular basis and was enjoying it. Katecia was turning into a young lady right before my eyes and Jeremiah was…let's just say he was still being Jeremiah.

Corey had a few commas in his life but had made it through them. He was living life and learning valuable lessons all at the same time. He was the one that led me to the church in Germany where I gave my life to the Lord, he was only 11 years old at the time. Though he went through the things he went though, I was confident that he would overcome every obstacle that he would face in life because of his foundation.

My grandma was still doing well. All nine of her children were still alive and doing well. She was blessed to have grandchildren, great grandchildren and 2 great-great grandchildren. There were 5 generations of Joyner women at that time. God had truly blessed us as a family.

My spiritual life was on the upside for the most part. My main problem by being at the Baptist Church was still proving to be the lack of accountability. Because the church was so large, I didn't know very many people. I was one of those people that loved to hide in the background instead of being in the forefront.

When a person like me is unsupervised, you can bet that they will fall off. My justification was that I didn't choose the life, the life chose me. No matter how hard I tried to escape, God always kept me on a short leash.

By the time May 2008 rolled around Katecia was living with her best friend. She had turned 18 back in November and was about to graduate from Central High School. Earlier in the year, Solathian and I agreed that he would take Jeremiah back to Germany with him so he could go to school there the 2008-2009 school year. Although I have much love for my son, I was greatly anticipating the move. Solathian and I agreed that Jeremiah would go back with him after Katecia's graduation.

Unfortunately, things didn't happen as planned. Before coming to Arkansas, Solathian called and informed me that he would not be able to take Jeremiah back with him. I could not believe that he was letting me down again. Do you remember when Jeremiah was 2 and I was working for the airlines? He agreed to keep him then but I ended up taking him back home with me. After I got off the phone with Solathian, I went outside where my oldest daughter Tashona was standing, smoking a cigarette—I asked her if I could have it.

Solathian came for the graduation and I was still upset with him because he reneged on our agreement. He was not one of my favorite people at that time but I was still cordial to him during his stay. I recall us watching T.V. one day when my cell phone rang. It was some guy and he asked me to speak to a female I didn't know. When I told him that he had the wrong number he asked me *my* name. I told him he had the wrong number again and hung up the phone. A few days later Solathian went back to Germany and I fed my stress with Grand Prix cigarettes—I was hooked again.

I started with one a day, then two a day, then a pack; they were cheap and they fed my cravings. It was the beginning of summer yet I was already feeling anxious about the next school year; I knew that Jeremiah was going to take me down through there once again. Due to my high stress levels, I was smoking more than I was eating and began to lose weight. I went from a size 10 to a size 8 and then finally to a size 6 which I had not been since I was probably 6, then down to a size 5.

One day as I was sitting on the front porch smoking, my phone rang. It was the same dude that called the week prior. He told me that his name was Jerry*. He begged me not to hang up and began to tell me about himself. Before long he was indulging me with very private details of his life. Things that you don't readily tell anyone and especially not anyone that you just met. It was something about his honesty that intrigued me. Besides his honesty, he was very funny. We were on the phone for over an hour talking and laughing—it was as if I had known him for years. For that one hour I didn't have a care in the world. It was such a relief to be able to finally laugh again.

Proverbs 15:13
"A merry heart maketh a cheerful countenance; but by sorrow of the heart the spirit is broken."

Don't Let the Devil Ride

*U*nfortunately, my discontentment with my circumstances led me right into the devil's lair (Jerry's lair) and I couldn't blame anyone but myself for hooking up with someone that had lunatic tendencies. Forgive me Lord because I know that's your child but OMG! That man was the business for real!! I wish I could share his real name in case one of you ladies reading this book should happen to run into him. I would tell you, RUN! HOP! SKIP! SPEED OFF! JUMP OFF! Do whatever you must do to get away! I quote the old-school church song that says *"don't let the devil ride, cause if you let him ride, he'll wanna drive"*. That song was telling the truth.

Jerry and I met up after about 2 weeks of talking on the phone. He was from ***** ****** ****and we met at a park. He started out being nice enough and could always make me laugh. He said he was brought up in church (heard that one before) but was no longer living the life (heard that too). He had a knack for coming up with unflattering names to call people and the things that came out of his mouth most times were crazy and harsh. On top of that, he was a drinker and not a casual drinker. I mean I'm eating cereal and he's drinking a 40-oz. type of drinker. Looking back, he wasn't the one acting like a lunatic, I was. Admitting you have a problem is the first step to recovery, remember that.

After about a month after we met, Jerry introduced me to his family—most of which were drinkers that had the same *tendencies* he had. After we had our first sexual encounter, I knew I was about to plummet to my spiritual demise. Mind you, I stopped going to church back when I started back smoking. I was always conscious of the fact that it was my job as God's mouthpiece to cause unbelievers to believe. When I wasn't in proper alignment to do that, I would pull a Jonah and head in the opposite direction.

Naturally, when I started being sexually active, sinning with Jerry, everything spiritual shut down in my life. I stopped reading, praying and fasting—*again*. Many nights I would hang out with Jerry in his city at one of his friends or relatives house and watch him gamble, drink and gamble some more. Although his drinking was a major problem, it was not his only problem. He did not work, but received a check (they should have given him two). There were times when he would become very belligerent and yell when he didn't get his way. He was also very jealous and needy. The thing that kept me with him so long was the soul tie. We were compatible only in the thing that strengthened our soul tie. It was what grandma from the Klumps referred to as *relations*.

Though intimacy was our bond, Jerry made me laugh when nothing else could. As crazy as it may sound, I cared for him and believed that he cared for me too. Although I felt the way I did about Jery, I knew that he could not and would not *ever, ever, ever* be my husband. Not even if he got saved, filled with the Holy Ghost and spoke in tongues in 5 different languages. My plan was to get back on track with God and help him find God again. About a year into the relationship, God showed me in a dream that it was all a set up.

In the dream, I was standing in my front yard and I noticed that the front door to my house was not fully closed. As I stood there, I saw one of my daughters and some other people standing in the yard talking. Suddenly, the front door opens and people start walking out of my house carrying furniture and TV's and I'm thinking to myself, what is going on? Does anyone see these people taking my stuff? Then I start wondering, why am I standing here watching them take my stuff? Eventually I walk up to the house and look inside and the tops of everything was missing. The sofa's base is there but the sofa itself is gone, bar stool legs are there but the seat is gone and tables only had legs. God spoke to me through that dream and said, "You have allowed the devil to come in but your foundation is still there".

There was no money coming in except money from a few broker price opinions that I was completing and child support so I applied for and got a part time job at Pulaski County Detention Center. It was there that I met a lady named Candy. She and I ended up being and still are good friends. Candy talked me through some times when I felt like jumping off a ledge and allowed me to vent to her whenever I needed to. I don't think she realized how important her friendship was to me during that time but she was the only one that seemed to understand the complicated relationship that Jerry and I shared and my love for God. She didn't judge me and I appreciated her for that.

I worked at the Detention Center for several months before my hours were cut and it became too much work for too little money. I decided to leave and began working part time at Fed-Ex. It was hard work with not a lot of hours but since my brook was dry and I needed the money, I did what a real "G" does—go hard in the paint. After all, I was back *out in them streets* and I knew more than God, right? if a hashtag were put behind that sentence it would read **#foolish.**

I continued to see Jerry despite the dream and paid the price dearly. No good time compared to the bad times that proceeded that good time. His mindset was like that of an 18-year-old although he was only a few years younger than me. He had no goals or dreams and could not think pass owning Jordan's and a car. Negro what about a house? A bank account? A J.O.B.? My children didn't care for him at all, especially Katecia. I believe if I would have given her the okay, she would've took him out herself. To put the icing on the cake, near the end of our relationship I found out he was cheating on me. I confronted him about the text message I heard come through on his phone one night. Someone was asking where he was and what time he was coming over. He claimed it was his cousin. Women trust your gut—it's not lying.

Weeks passed and then "she" called me one day. I was like Nene from Real Housewives, "you done lost your *! @#$% mind". Remember I'm in a backslidden state and I'm buck. She was telling me that she and Jerry met at some hole in the wall club and that they had been talking for a while. He claimed she was stalking him. I was like "really? you that big of a catch that somebody stalking you? If you don't get outta my house you horse mouth $%#^&*^ &*^$^%#@!" See that's what happens when you think *you* can convert somebody, they end up converting you. His harsh words became my harsh words.

In February, the venue my sister had reserved for her husband's birthday party fell through so I volunteered to let her have the party at my house. Though it was s last minute change, the word got around and lots of people showed up—including Jerry. There were card games, dancing and lots of drinking. People were standing outside smoking and cars were parked up and down both sides of the street. There were people that were invited and even a few that we don't know who they were to this day. I wasn't doing a lot of drinking but the little buzz I had quickly left as I stood outside with my sister and cousins. I will never forget; my cousin Jackie was home from Atlanta and I was standing outside smoking a cigarette. She walked up and stopped in her tracks when she saw the cigarette in my hand. She said "Twana smoking… and got a boyfriend? The devil is busy!" Although we all laughed, it really wasn't funny. The very thing I had been trying to avoid happened anyway, my witness had been compromised.

After the party, Jerry left with one of his homeboys. It was that night that I decided to take the advice of a country singer named Kenny Rogers. Kenny says, "you got to know when to hold em', know when to fold em', know when to walk away, and know when to run…." I chose the latter. I did not see or speak to Jerry for weeks. By the time that I accepted his call, my mind was in a better place and I was calling out his lies. (*It ain't no fun when the rabbit got the gun.*)

While closing that chapter in my life, the soul tie still had me. I was still thinking about him, wanting to be with him (sexually), crying in the middle of the night, wondering where he was—it was crazzzzzzzy! Glory be to God for the church. I got that little Acura in gear one Sunday and headed right back into the house of the Lord! I prayed and asked God to deliver me from the foolishness I had entangled myself in. I asked Him to return Jerry's spirit to him and to return my spirit to me. I knew that was the only way that the soul tie could be broken. It wasn't easy, but I began to take baby steps toward my deliverance. Just as I was getting my stride back, in stepped my next test… I call it "the giant".

1 Corinthians 15:33 (NIV)
"Do not be misled: bad company corrupts good character"

Taking down the Giant

I was still working part time at Fed-Ex when this very tall guy came in and started working with us. He came through a temp agency and was a very polite, nice guy. A couple of months after meeting and working together *Calvin asked me to go to lunch. During our conversation, I found out that we were both born in the month of February. Though our birthdays were only one day apart, our ages were years apart. This was a problem for me because he didn't seem seasoned enough. On the other hand he liked older women because they were seasoned. Trouble from the start.

I went through the motions of dating Calvin for several months. I was the shot caller and knew exactly what I was doing. My self-esteem was not low, I wasn't trying to fill a void, I was merely passing time. All the while I was secretly disgusted with the state of my life. Calvin was a very thoughtful and caring guy and my family liked him. He loved my grandbaby Davine' Joi, (Katecia's baby that was born in 2009) and spoiled her rotten. He was a good guy, just not my type of guy.

He and I were both taking classes at the community college when he told me that he enlisted and had been accepted into the military. I must admit that I was a bit disappointed that he waited until after the fact to tell me—one of his main faults was secrecy. He wasn't very open about his past and often acted and then told me about it later. Therefore it came as no surprise when he was forced to tell me that his baby mama lived around the corner from me. One day we were leaving my house and this lady pulled up beside us and stopped. Without even speaking, she began yelling at him, telling him what she was going to do to their daughter for acting up at school and without letting him speak, sped off down the street. I'm sitting there like what in the world is going on here? He began fast talking and told me that the two of them did not get along very well and that she often used their daughter's misbehavior as an excuse to talk bad to him. Then he hit me with the okey-doke and told me that she lived in the apartments around the corner from me. This meant that she had been seeing his vehicle at my house for months. Thank goodness that she wasn't a crazy woman because she could have walked up to me and shot me and I would not have been the wiser as to who she was. Because he wasn't man enough to tell me that his baby's mama lived practically in my backyard, I stopped trusting him completely. Every word that came out of his mouth, I considered a lie. All the no—goods I dated previously had taught me not to trust after the first lie.

Jerry was still calling me every now and then trying to reconcile. Finally just out of curiosity, I agreed to meet up with him one day at a park. It only took a few brief minutes to realize that I was truly over him. He mentioned that he had rode through my neighborhood and saw "the giant" at my house. As he questioned me about him, I got in my car and never looked back. I laughed all the way home thinking how delusional I had been to allow him in my life. I must admit, he got one last laugh out of me with that "giant" comment. It wasn't the last time I saw Jerry but it was the most memorable. Old Jerry, if I could have taken his mouth and cleaned it out with soap, gave him a new brain and a new attitude, put him in AA and convinced them to give him 2 checks—he could've been the one…

It was around March or April of 2010 that God began to deal with me a lot more. I knew that just as in times past, my chain was about to be yanked. This time He not only dealt with me about my lifestyle but also about the journal that I had been working on for 7 years. God was telling me that He wanted me to turn my journal into a book. I retrieved the cd that held my life story from its hiding place and began to read all the intimate and revealing things that I shared. I was like nah, this can't be God telling me to do this… this is the devil trying to get me to put all my business out there so people can look at me crazy and judge me. I thought it was a setup—my punishment for backsliding and fornicating. I put the cd back in its safe place and dismissed the thought.

It seemed like the more that I tried to dismiss the thought of turning my journal into a book, the more that God kept dealing with me about it. I started doing my research and found out that copyrighting your work is one of the first things that a person should do to protect it. Although my journal read like a book already, it was not exactly in book format. I wanted it to be protected in case it fell into the wrong hands so I went online and paid the fee to copyright it. After I got my confirmation number a few seconds later, I tucked it and the cd safely away again.

It was July 2, 2010 and we had just celebrated my grandmother's 90th birthday earlier that day. It had become a family tradition to throw grandma a huge birthday party each year on or near her July 6th birthday. I don't recall where we were the first time, but I do know that the second time that Calvin asked me to marry him was that day on my grandmother's porch in front of my brother, his wife and some friends of the family. I was totally embarrassed and he was totally serious as he got down on one knee and proposed. I played it off by saying something funny and everyone laughed. Then I whispered in his ear to stop embarrassing me and told him to get off his knee. Everyone thought that he was only joking but I knew that he wasn't. Things between the two of us had moved quickly when we first met because I was on the rebound from Jerry. He was good company back then and such a caring guy. Fortunately, it didn't take me long to realize that he wasn't the guy I wanted to spend the rest of my life with. Honestly, if Jerry had Calvin's heart and caring spirit, Jerry would have been husband #4. The fact of the matter is you can't change the core of a person no matter how hard you try, only God can do that.

I began to share with Calvin how God was dealing with me about my lifestyle (fornicating) and how I was feeling led to publish a book about my life. He was encouraging concerning the book, but dismissive concerning life style changes. I figured I could show him better than I could tell him so I began to cut him off. When I did that, the real Calvin began to emerge and I didn't like him. That Calvin didn't want me to deny my flesh because he didn't want to deny his flesh. I knew he was about to get kicked permanently to the curb when he started coming to my house drunk. I didn't even know he drank! He was entirely too tall to be drunk because he looked like a swaying pole. I knew then that it was time for me to tighten up my back stroke. I had finally grown weary with myself and with Calvin.

I was on my 5th second chance and yet God stood with open

arms, welcoming me back to him. He let me know that no man was going to take His place in my life and certainly not one that did not serve Him. Just like the harlot Gomer—the Prophet Hosea's wife, God began to hedge me in so that I would not be able to leave Him again and go after my lovers.

Titus 2:14

"Who gave himself for us, that he might redeem us from all iniquity, and purify unto himself a peculiar people, zealous of good works."

He saw the Best in Me

February 2011 came and I decided to treat myself to a special gift, A Yorkie puppy. I had not had a pet since Puddles and you all know what happened to Puddles. After searching the paper, I saw that Yorkies did not come cheap but since I had a little extra tax refund money, I decided to splurge a little bit. I finally ran across an ad placed by a lady in North Little Rock that had Yorkies for a reasonable price. I called her and we agreed to meet that Saturday at Kohls. I was shelling out a lot of money so I asked Corey to ride along with me, just in case.

When we arrived at Kohls, we saw a SUV with the hatch raised and a lady carefully handling 3 of the most beautiful black and brown puppies with big blue bows around their necks. I was finding it hard to decide which one I wanted until I noticed that one kept trying to get to me. The more the lady tried to hold him back, the more he came towards me. I knew that he was the one. On the way home Corey and I brainstormed on what to name him. Corey finally came up with the name Kohl. His logic of course was that we bought him from the lady at Kohls...

Solathian was still in Germany and had met someone along the way. We found out on Facebook that she was the new "Mrs. Nuniss". Isn't it amazing the things you can find out on Facebook? Once the dust settled and they were done honeymooning, he agreed to let Jeremiah stay with him and his new wife and stepson in Germany. His past record was not reassuring so I took it with a grain of salt. It was not until he called me with the flight information that I was sure that Jeremiah was really going. I was a little hesitant about letting Jeremiah travel all the way to Germany alone. Although he was flying accompanied, I was afraid he might accidentally get left somewhere. Trust me, stranger things had happened. I finally prayed about it and got peace. Calvin and I drove him to the airport in Memphis a couple of weeks later. As I stood and watched my baby boy board the plane to what I hoped would be a life changing experience for him, I cried.

Calvin was about to leave for the Army and I must say I was both happy and sad. Overall, he was a good person with skeletons in his closet like everyone else. My skeletons and his skeletons were proving to be too many skeletons so I decided that I just wanted to be friends. With Calvin there was no middle ground; either we would be a couple or nothing at all. He gave me an ultimatum but ended up making the decision for me when he appeared on my doorstep drunk again. He got on my nerves so bad that night that I put him out of my house. He tried to reason with me as I led him to his car, but I wasn't having it. As we were walking, I happened to look up into the sky and the clouds looked scary and extremely low. It was a weird night and got a bit weirder when Calvin realized that I was ignoring him and left spinning tires in a car that was about the length of my block. Needless to say, that was the end of Calvin.

With more than enough time on my hands, I began to pour myself into putting the book together. I researched and consulted with a young lady named Jennifer Black who gave me great pointers and even hooked me up with a consultant. The consultant advised me on self-publishing and gave me contacts for editors and cover designers. We went into contract shortly thereafter and he was the first one to read my rough draft.

Though I still had a way to go, he thought that my story would make a great book. He felt that teenagers and young adults would especially benefit.

As I worked on the book, God worked on me. Spiritually I was becoming stronger and seeking Him more. I totally relied on the fact that I knew His voice and that I was doing as I was told. The Holy Spirit led me through the process of piecing my life together chronologically for the book. He also gave me the name of the publishing company that God would have me to form. I was led to self-publish the book and to name my company *God's Way Publishing*.

According to the world's standards, I was a failure. I didn't have a fancy house or fancy car. I didn't have stable income and had gone from pillar to post for years. Fortunately for me, God's standards are not man's standards because He didn't view me as a failure. God planned to use every bad relationship, every ounce of weed, every time I was homeless and every time I thought I got away from Him in a way that I never imagined. He planned for it to "work out for my good."

There is a popular song by Marvin Sapp that says, "He saw the *best* in me, when everyone else around me could only see the *worst* in me". Many of the awesome, life changing gifts that God has placed inside of us cannot be fully revealed until *He's ready* for us to make our debut.

Ephesians 2:10
"For we are his workmanship, created in Christ Jesus unto good works, which God hath before ordained that we should walk in them."

Torn

I tried to ignore the call, but I could hear it so plain. The more I resisted, the louder it became. God was telling me that it was time for me to make a choice. I was torn between the two—God's will for my life and my will. Spirit vs Flesh. It was time for me to choose—God's Way—straight paths or my way-crooked paths. To help me out, God strategically used the journals to open my eyes to the reality of who I was at my core. The journal laid out my life in black and white. Right before my eyes lay the good, the bad and the ugly. As my words stared me in the face, I had no choice but to own them. The day God forced me to look at the journals objectively was the day that everything came full circle.

Being a writer had been my dream as a young girl; 30 years later my dream was about to come to fruition. I was finally going to be able to exercise the gift that God had placed inside of me. Because I was *destined* to write, my life was about to become my ministry.

I began to throw myself wholeheartedly into turning my journal into the book that God had predestined. The book became not only my therapy but my way of escape. I could feel the walls being torn down in my life as I became naked and unashamed before God. I slowly relinquished my will and allowed Him to redeem and expose me by my own hand until He could see a reflection of Himself in me. Surprisingly, the liberation I began to feel helped fuel my desire to share my story with others. I wanted everyone that read my story to see that sometimes we can be our own worst enemy and that in some instances we must be crushed in order for our anointing to flow.

One day as I sat at my computer I pulled up the journal to see how far I had gotten. What started out as a few pages, was over 100 pages and covered the most intimate and private experiences of my life. I asked the Lord what he wanted me to do. He said "publish it". I said Lord, how? "He said "I will show you". I asked what will I call it? He said *Looking for Love in all the Wrong Places*. Just like that, in eight words, God summed up the first 30 years of my life. He gave me a starting point and an ending point—the Holy Spirit gave me the rest. In that moment of time, it became apparent that though salvation is free to us because Jesus paid the price on the cross, the anointing is going to cost us something.

I was reading over a chapter in the journal entitled "summertime" when fear came over me and I digressed. After reading it, I no longer wanted to share my deepest, darkest secrets with the world. I was quickly reminded that when you expose yourself, you make yourself vulnerable to those you expose yourself to. I began to wonder, what will my family think? What will my children think? What will my friends think? That's when God showed me His will through His Word.

Revelations 12:11 says *"And they overcame him by the blood of the Lamb, and by the word of their testimony; and they loved not their lives unto the death."* God was telling me through that scripture that not only would my story benefit others, it would benefit me the most. I knew that if I didn't succumb to what God was telling me to do, the blood would be required at my hands just like he warned the Prophet Ezekiel in Ezekiel 3:18.

When the thought of it all became too overwhelming, I prayed a prayer that went something like this: "Dear Lord, I know that you chose me from my mother's womb to be a mouthpiece for you. Create in me a clean heart and renew a right spirit within me. Renew my mind so that I will not battle with the enemy-in-me. Show me Lord what lies at the root of my issues so that I can denounce it. Lord I surrender myself to you, please give me the courage and the boldness to do what you have called me to do. In Jesus name, Amen"

When I prayed that prayer of surrender, I did not know the highs and the extreme lows that I was about to suffer for His sake. I did not know that He was about to use my life to bring Himself glory. I also did not know that once I experienced my mountaintop experience that I would experience a valley experience that would almost take me out completely spiritually.

There were times in my life that it appeared that God had forgotten all about me, but in actuality His eyes were always on me. He watched over me as he held me over an open flame, adjusting the temperature only slightly so that my sins would not kill me. Just like a silversmith, He was determined not to remove me from the flame until He could see His reflection in me.

I once heard a minister say "My greatest sermon will not be preached with my lips, my greatest sermon will be preached with my life." I finally understood what he meant. I thought I had been through it all and that my dark days were behind me. I did not realize that it gets even darker right before dawn…

Jeremiah 18:4

"And the vessel that he made of clay was marred in the hand of the potter: so, he made it again another vessel, as seemed good to the potter to make it."

Other Books/ Works by This Author

Books
The Trilogy

Looking For Love in All the Wrong Places	pt. 1	2011
Torn Between Two Lovers	pt. 2	2017

Coming Soon:

Developed in a Dark Room	pt. 3	2017/18

Other Works

Looking for Love in all the Wrong Places-The Skit
Looking for Love in all the Wrong Places-The Play
2013/2014

Twana Nuniss	**Sabrina Wright**
Producer	**Director/playwright**

Books Available on Amazon.com

About the Author

Twana Joyner-Nuniss is an Evangelist, Author and Entrepreneur. She is the mother of four children and nana to 10 grandchildren. She is the author of *Looking for Love in all the Wrong Places* and the producer of Looking for Love-The Play, written and directed by Sabrina Wright of So Wright Productions. *Twana was first inspired to write Looking for Love in 2010 and was given a mandate to write two additional books in order to comprise a trilogy of her life experiences.* She is owner of Nuniss Realty, God's Way Publishing and founder/overseer of My Brother's Keeper Outreach.

Twana speaking on *Torn between Two Lovers*:

"After moving back to the Unites States I found myself alone and in a spiritual tug of war. The more I tried to convince myself that I was one hundred percent committed to God, the more that I found myself in compromising positions. I doubted my salvation and my faith. I felt like a complete screw up most times; I could not fully discern the anointing that other people saw and found it difficult to walk in the purpose that was predetermined for my life.

God restored my love for writing and through writing the first book, I realized that I not only had a love for it, but it was the gift God wanted me to share with the world. I pray that my testimony will win souls to the Kingdom and bring Him the glory He deserves.

There were times by all accounts that I should have been dead, but nothing was able to abort the purpose of me being here nor negate the fact that God chose me to do a work for Him. I love the teachings of the late great Myles Munroe. There was something that he said that has stuck with me over the years, he said "don't die old, die empty". That is now my prayer."

Part 3 of the trilogy is in the works. There are also future plans to write Christian inspired children's books, publish a Singles Ministry Series and executive produce **Looking For Love-The Movie.**

Galatians 5:16, 17

"I say then; Walk in the Spirit and you shall not fulfill the lust of the flesh. For the flesh lusts against the Spirit, and the Spirit against the flesh; and these are contrary to one another, so that you do not do the things that you wish.

Made in the USA
Lexington, KY
09 November 2019

56589441R00105